How to be
a happy
non-smoker

ARCTURUS

Published by Arcturus Canada
A division of Arcturus Publishing Limited
26/27 Bickels Yard,151-153 Bermondsey Street
London SE1 3HA

ISBN-13: 978-1-905555-05-5
ISBN-10: 1-905555-05-9

British Library Cataloguing-in-Publication Data:a catalogue record
for this book is available from the British Library

This edition printed in 2006
Text copyright © 2005 Allen Carr's Easyway (International) Limited
Design copyright © 2005 Arcturus Publishing Limited

Typeset by MATS

Printed in England

CONTENTS

INTRODUCTION

Most smokers are convinced that it is difficult to stop smoking. The problem, we're told, is the enormous amount of willpower it takes to resist the craving to light up.

Wouldn't it be marvellous then not to have this battle of wills, and to be able to stop easily? The good news is that there is an easy way, a way by which any smoker can quit immediately and permanently, without using willpower, suffering withdrawal symptoms, needing substitutes or even putting on weight. I know you might find this difficult to accept, but it's true. I've been proving it for over twenty years, not only with my books, but also at my worldwide network of clinics.

Not surprisingly, I call my method Easyway. My name is Allen Carr, and I am regarded as the world's leading expert on helping smokers quit. I can help you, by showing you that our ideas and beliefs about smoking are based on mis-information and illusions, and that once you see through them you will be free forever.

My text can be used in whatever way you choose. Some readers will like the calendar structure, whereas others might want to read the text in just a few sittings. The decision when to stop is yours alone and entirely personal. Don't think you have to wait until 31 December if you want to stop earlier. You decide when you want to smoke that final cigarette.

This book will provide you with an inspiring companion and enable you to do it – easily, painlessly, and permanently. I am so confident of your success that, if you fail to stop smoking with this book, you can recover its cost, in the form of a discount, if you attend one of my clinics, listed at the end. So let me be your guide to stopping smoking enjoyably, and becoming what every smoker wants to be – a happy non-smoker.

JANUARY

1 January

New Year's Day! The day every smoker resolves to stop smoking. Don't! For reasons I will explain later, it just happens to be the very worst day in the year, and your chances of success are less than one in a hundred unless careful preparation has been made. Instead let this be the first day of an exciting adventure: the day you start preparing yourself to quit easily, immediately and permanently. **But please do not attempt to stop or even try to cut down until I advise you to do so.**

2 January

Imagine waking up one morning and thinking: 'I know it's very difficult but I'm going to try to climb Mount Everest today.' The biggest fool on earth wouldn't believe they could succeed without months of careful preparation. Any smoker can find it easy, even enjoyable, to quit immediately and permanently. But without careful preparation it'll be like climbing Mount Everest.

3 January

You could spend a lifetime trying to break into a safe. But if you know the correct combination, opening the safe is easy. The nicotine trap is the most subtle, ingenious confidence trick that Mother Nature and mankind have contrived to lay. This little book contains the key – the correct combination to the safe – that will allow you to escape from the trap. **All you have to do is to follow a few simple instructions.**

4 January

Most smokers start their attempt at quitting feeling like a lamb being led to slaughter. **Your first instruction is to cast away all feelings of doom and gloom.** Stopping smoking is probably the best decision you'll ever make. You have so much to gain. The very worst thing that can happen is that you'll fail, in which case you will have lost nothing. So see the situation in its true light and enjoy the process of your escape from the nicotine trap. The beautiful truth is: I have nothing but good news for you.

5 January

Are you still apprehensive about quitting? Don't worry, this is quite normal. All smokers have a permanent tug-of-war going on inside their brains. On the bad side – fear: it's ruining my health and wealth. By this token every smoker wishes they'd never started. On the good side, smoking is a pleasure, a friend, a crutch. When these ideas are fixed on, every smoker wants to continue to smoke.

6 January

In reality, the good side is also about fear: will I be able to enjoy social occasions or be able to concentrate or cope with stress without a cigarette? If you've previously tried to quit using willpower, you will know what a miserable experience it can be. I know it's difficult to imagine life without cigarettes, but I promise you that, with my method, soon the only mystery left will be why you ever felt the need to light a cigarette, and you'll look at other smokers with pity rather than envy. So keep cheerful. You are about to achieve something marvellous.

7 January

Even if you have only half a brain you will already have realized that smoking is a filthy, disgusting and nowadays decidedly anti-social pastime that isn't good either for your health or your finances. If you are expecting me to give graphic details about the damage smoking does to your body, or to lecture you on your stupidity in continuing to smoke, you will be disappointed.

8 January

I know that the so-called experts and our families continually remind us of these things. I'm also aware that these are probably the main reasons that you wish to stop. But it never seems to occur to these 'experts', or ourselves for that matter, that we don't smoke for the reasons we shouldn't. If you want to quit, the real problem is to remove the reasons that make you want or need a cigarette.

9 January

Perhaps you think you know those reasons: that smoking relaxes you and relieves nerves and stress, aids concentration and relieves boredom. Or perhaps you like the taste and smell of cigarettes. Or perhaps you've sunk to the stage that I once did. I couldn't think of a single advantage of smoking, and believed I smoked either because I had an addictive personality, or because it was a habit I couldn't break.

10 January

Now I have some exceedingly good news for you. In reality, you get no pleasure or crutch from smoking, and neither does any other smoker. What's more, smoking actually impedes relaxation and concentration, and increases boredom, stress and nervousness.

11 January

'It's something to do with my hands,' people say. Like a nervous twitch? Some people drum their fingers or tap the table-top when nervous, agitated, anxious, stressed or bored. A smoker apparently needs to handle a cigarette. But it doesn't stop at just holding it, playing with it and then putting it back in the packet. If it did, by now you would still be on your second cigarette.

12 January

You would not have lit that cigarette if it were really true that you wanted something to keep your hands occupied. Similarly, you would never have felt uptight or agitated if your true need was simply to touch a cigarette. You could just as easily — and less expensively — handle a stick or a pencil instead.

13 January

'It's something to put in my mouth.' Like a comforter or a dummy? Something that makes you feel secure, like sucking your thumb as a child? No one puts an unlit cigarette in their mouth just to soothe their nerves, to help them relax or enjoy an occasion. Instinctively we know there are better ways of coping. We have the ability to cope with most of life's problems, but we may have forgotten how to do so. Don't worry, the knowledge will come back.

14 January

Your second instruction is to open your mind. Have you ever met a narrow-minded person, whose mind is as impenetrable as a giant clam? Of course you have. With the exception of you and me, the entire human race is made up of such people! However, I'll guarantee that you've never met a single person who admitted to being narrow-minded. The instruction to open your mind is simple enough. Following it is another matter. But your success depends upon you doing so.

15 January

My claims might appear somewhat exaggerated. But before you dismiss them, let's take a look at the counter-claims, i.e. the ways in which cigarettes are supposed to help you. Relaxation and stress are complete opposites. So are boredom and concentration. If I tried to sell you a magic pill that had completely the opposite effect to an identical pill taken an hour earlier, would you be stupid enough to buy it?

'To do the same thing again and again and expect different results is madness.' Albert Einstein.

16 January

Little wonder smokers are reluctant to stop and find it very difficult! Or that we think of cigarettes as our little pleasure, friend and crutch, that are there for us at the most significant times of our lives – when we are relaxing, concentrating, nervous, bored or under stress. What other times are there, except, of course, when we are asleep or eating, and many smokers have to smoke even while they are eating.

17 January

From birth our society brainwashes us not only to believe cigarettes are magic pills, but also that they actually smell and taste good. Taste good! Where does taste come into it? We don't eat cigarettes, and if you tried you'd be violently sick! The fact is that when we smoke cigarettes we adapt to the blended concoctions put in them. Nicotine, in its base form, is harsh and acrid. The tobacco companies mask its true flavour by blending it with 'softeners' such as chocolate, vanilla, honey, molasses, and, of course, menthol. Each country has special blends to reflect the taste buds of its inhabitants; France, for example, has *Gitanes*.

18 January

Fortunately, most smokers can remember their first experimental puffing at cigarettes, how foul they tasted and how hard they had to work in order to inhale without feeling sick or having a coughing fit. Did we really work so hard just to acquire the taste? If you believe so, light a cigarette now. Deliberately take six deep, consecutive drags and concentrate on the taste. Ask yourself what's so pleasurable about inhaling filthy, cancer-inducing fumes into your lungs throughout your life, and having to pay a huge amount for the privilege.

19 January

You might say, 'I enjoy the feeling of inhaling the smoke and getting a hit.' The human body is not designed to inhale smoke. If you are burning garden waste or even barbecuing, you don't hover over the smoke to 'enjoy' inhaling it. We choke if we inhale smoke. Where does this sense of enjoyment come from? It comes courtesy of the manufacturers. Cigarettes have had important ingredients added which prevent you from choking. These are glycerol and ethyl alcohol. When burnt incandescently they disperse as tiny droplets of vapour which, when they are inhaled, coat the back of the throat. The alcohol acts as a mild anaesthetic, and the glycerol stops the throat from drying out.

20 January

You might argue that on certain occasions tobacco smoke does smell good. I cannot argue with that. But you'll find this only happens when you are craving a cigarette and never when you are actually smoking one. I love the smell of a rose but I've never had any desire to dry the leaves, wrap them in paper, set light to them and inhale the fumes.

21 January

In fact, as you will soon prove to yourself, practically every supposed benefit of smoking that we have been brainwashed to believe from birth, is the direct opposite to reality. However, all the facts on the down side are true! Imagine each of these false beliefs as a number on the combination lock you need in order to escape from the nicotine trap. There are over 20 of these false conceptions. Little wonder that smokers find it difficult, if not impossible, to stop. We are going to explode these myths. **But first we must deal with your final instruction.**

22 January

One of the great aspects about Easyway that our clients most appreciate is that you can continue to smoke during the process of becoming a non-smoker. With a 'willpower' method – i.e. any method other than Easyway – you quit first and hope that one day the craving to smoke will cease. But how can you test the truth about smoking if you no longer smoke?

23 January

If you believe that you get some genuine pleasure and/or help from smoking, why should you change that belief once you stop? **In a sense I've already given you your final instruction: I've asked you to continue to smoke until I advise you otherwise.** But there's a little more to it than that , and it's part of the mind-opening process. Most 20-a-day smokers freely admit that they only enjoy about two of the cigarettes they smoke each day. This begs the question: why do we bother to smoke the remainder if we don't enjoy them? We cannot think of a logical reason for this paradox so we come up with an excuse: it's just habit.

24 January

The reality is that we don't enjoy any of the cigarettes we smoke. We smoke the vast majority of the cigarettes subconsciously. Earlier I asked you to consciously take six deep, consecutive drags and concentrate on the taste. **If we consciously smoked every cigarette,** not only would there be no pleasure in breathing filthy fumes into our lungs, but we would also realize that we were spending a fortune and that this cigarette might just be the one to trigger lung cancer. If this were the case, no way would we light it, let alone suffer the illusion that we enjoyed it! But still we feel that we have to keep on doing it, so we close our minds to the reality.

25 January

But isn't it an established fact that certain cigarettes taste better than others – the one after a meal, for example? No, it's just part of the brainwashing. How can one identical cigarette out of the same packet taste different to another? You need to use this preparation period to discover the truth. **Consciously smoke the cigarette after a meal and at any other time when you think it tastes good.** In due course I will explain why certain cigarettes appear to taste better or to be more enjoyable than others.

26 January

You need to use this preparation period not just to discover the truth about your own smoking, but to see behind the façade of other smokers. What gets us hooked in the first place? The short answer is all the other people who smoke. But surely, you're probably asking yourself, they wouldn't do it unless they got some genuine help or pleasure from it? What hooks us is that the first cigarette tastes awful. Any fears we might have had that we too might spend a fortune as a slave to nicotine for the rest of our lives is quickly dispelled. 'How could anyone get hooked on these filthy things?' So we persevere, and before we know it, we are buying our own cigarettes and getting into a panic if we're running low!

27 January

Incredibly, society generally and smokers themselves believe they are smoking because they choose to smoke. This is the first major illusion that we are going to explode. It's not difficult to understand how the myth arose. After all, since nobody but ourselves forces us to smoke, isn't it obvious that we only do so because we choose to?

28 January

When did you choose to become a smoker? No, I don't mean when did you have your first experimental cigarettes. I mean when did you decide that you would buy your own cigarettes and smoke not just at social occasions but at other times, too, and would feel insecure without a packet to hand? When did you decide that you couldn't enjoy a meal without a cigarette, or answer the phone without a cigarette? If you've opened your mind, you'll discover that you never did.

29 January

It may comfort you to know that no smoker, living or dead, actually chose to become a smoker. It is only the belief that we are missing out on something that lures us into the trap. And even when we realize that we've been conned and manage to escape from the trap, it is only other smokers that make us feel deprived. Get it clearly into your mind that every smoker on the planet wishes they were a non-smoker. You might find this difficult to believe, but look at the facts …

30 January

We could all enjoy life and cope with it before we started smoking. The average 20-a-day smoker spends £50,000 over their lifetime risking developing several fatal and horrendous diseases. We spend half our lives smoking subconsciously wishing we didn't need to, and the other half feeling miserable because society won't allow us to smoke in certain situations. What sort of hobby is it that, when we are allowed to do it, we wish we didn't, and only when we aren't allowed to do it, does it seem precious? The biggest idiot on earth wouldn't choose to be in that situation!

31 January

In case you are still not convinced, try this one. Smokers will spend hours telling you about the great benefits they receive from smoking, but there's not a parent in western society who doesn't vehemently discourage their children or grand-children from smoking. Isn't this proof positive that they wished they themselves hadn't fallen into the trap?

FEBRUARY

1 February

Let's begin the second month by summarizing the lessons of the first:

- There's nothing pleasant about breathing cancerous fumes into your lungs.

- Neither you nor any other smoker smokes because you choose to do so, but because you fell into an ingenious trap that you don't know how to escape from.

2 February

Perhaps you are still not convinced that smokers smoke not because they choose to, but because they are the victim of a confidence trick. If so, then consider this: most smokers decide to try and quit at least once in their lives. That is a conscious and logical decision, that they would rather spend the rest of their lives as non-smokers than as smokers. If they smoke again it is not because they choose to, but because they failed to escape from the trap.

3 February

You might argue that some smokers have never attempted to quit and are therefore smoking purely because they choose to. If you are one of those smokers, you will know that they are smoking not because they choose to, but because they fear life without nicotine.

4 February

Not only has not one single person chosen to become a smoker, but the fear of being without nicotine is so great, and so obsessed are we with searching for any excuse to continue smoking, we seem completely oblivious to the sheer slavery of being a smoker. One of the ingenious aspects of the trap is that you can be in it for years before realizing you are hooked. Another is that even when you do realize it, you want to escape, but not today – always tomorrow.

5 February

Society tends to regard smokers as being somewhat stupid. Paradoxically, intelligent smokers also regard themselves as stupid. But if smokers are stupid people, it means that at any one time 90 per cent of the male population of western society was stupid. This includes men such as Einstein, Freud and Winston Churchill.

6 February

Because such smokers believe that smoking is stupid and cannot understand why they continue to smoke, they believe, just as I did, that it's because they have an addictive personality, or that they have some flaw in their genes, or because smoking is a habit and habits are difficult to break.

These are not so much reasons for smoking, as excuses for not being able to quit.

7 February

There is no such thing as an addictive personality. If I had a gregarious personality, it would mean that I wanted to mix with other people. It follows that if I had an addictive personality, I would want to be addicted, not just to nicotine, but also to heroin and any other addictive drug. Yet far from having addictive personalities, heavy smokers tend not to dabble with other drugs. It's the nicotine that's addictive, not your personality.

8 February

The 'flaw in your genes' argument is far more difficult to dispel. The 20th century was dominated by searching for pills to solve problems. Mankind cannot create a single living cell, yet the current trend is to blame our genes, as if the incredible intelligence that created the human body a billion times more sophisticated than any man-made machine has made a mistake. This is rather like dropping your watch from a great height and blaming the designer because it won't work.

9 February

When something goes wrong with a man-made product we trace the cause to its source and correct it. But with something as sophisticated as the human body, even when we know the cause of the problem – like smoking and over-eating – instead of solving the problem at source, we search for pills or blame our genes. It's akin to substituting a six-inch nail for a fuse and believing you've solved an electrical problem!

10 February

Once you understand the nicotine trap and have successfully escaped from it, you will realize that you weren't smoking because you have an addictive personality, or a suicidal complex, or some flaw in your genes. You will know that you were just another of the billions that fell into this ingenious trap and didn't know how to escape from it. This isn't a question of positive thinking – it's about knowledge and understanding. You cannot win a battle unless you are fully prepared and know your enemy's weakness.

11 February

So far I haven't proved to you that you derive no benefits whatsoever from smoking. However, if you have opened your mind and studied your own smoking and observed other smokers, you will already have proved to yourself that the facts about smoking that society perpetuates even to this day, are grossly distorted. So why is it we genuinely believe that the cigarette is the magic pill that will enhance every situation?

12 February

Have you ever wondered how anyone can have such a distorted view of life that they believe they actually enjoy sticking a hypodermic syringe into a vein? Heroin addicts do! Why do you think they do that? Society led me to believe that they do it to enjoy wonderful dreams.

13 February

When you go to bed at night, are you particularly bothered that you won't have marvellous dreams? Or are you like me: just hoping that you won't have nightmares and will get a good night's sleep? Do you believe anyone would be stupid enough to go through the misery of being a heroin addict just to have marvellous dreams?

14 February

Now imagine a heroin addict with no heroin – the misery, the panic. Then try to visualize the relief they feel when they are allowed to inject a shot of heroin into a vein. Non-heroin addicts don't experience that panic feeling. Each shot of heroin, far from relieving that feeling, merely causes it!

15 February

Non-smokers are in exactly the same position – they don't have to go searching for a late-night garage when they get low on cigarettes. Neither did you before you fell into the nicotine trap. Non-smokers see smokers just as you would see a heroin addict or an alcoholic – someone whose life is being dominated by an addictive drug. Nicotine conveniently avoids being classified as a drug as it is a poison. It is now the world's number one lethal, addictive over-the-counter product, and yet it is perfectly legal.

16 February

So how is it that, before we fall into the trap, we see smoking as a filthy, disgusting habit and smokers as somewhat pathetic people who feel the need to spend a fortune just to breathe cancerous fumes into their lungs? Then, once we've fallen into the trap, we search for any excuse to remain in it, no matter how illogical that excuse might be?

17 February

Don't underestimate the ingenuity of the nicotine trap. It has already killed more people than all our wars have. But the nicotine trap is a confidence trick. Intelligent people fall for confidence tricks as well as stupid people. If you can see through a confidence trick, no way will you continue to fall for it.

18 February

If you could explain to a mouse exactly how a mouse-trap works, if it could understand that, if it attempted to nibble the cheese, a great steel bar would come crashing down and break its back, do you think the mouse would have gone anywhere near that piece of cheese in the first place?

19 February

If smokers knew that every time they breathed nicotine into their lungs, they would be paying a lot of money to risk developing horrendous diseases, but also making themselves more nervous, lacking in confidence, lethargic, less able to relax or concentrate or cope with stress, do you think they would continue to smoke?

20 February

Have you ever considered why it should be difficult to stop smoking? After all, no one forces us to smoke. So if we decide we don't want to smoke ever again, why should it be a problem? We don't have to take any positive action. We just have to refrain from lighting another cigarette. The so-called experts give three main reasons.

21 February

The first is that smoking is a habit and habits are difficult to break. Are they? I've been in the habit of driving on the left side of the road for over half a century, but when I drive on the continent I have no difficulty whatsoever in breaking that habit. In reality we don't do anything out of habit.

22 February

What is a habit? It is nothing more or less than repetition of a certain pattern of behaviour. How many times must you repeat certain behaviour before it becomes a habit? The number is immaterial, but let's assume it's five times. The first four times you repeated that behaviour you weren't doing so out of habit. The point I'm making is this: since you didn't repeat the behaviour four times out of habit, there must have been another reason for repeating it. In other words, it only became a habit because you had a reason to repeat it and not vice versa.

23 February

The reason some behaviours become habits is obvious. I was only in the habit of driving on the left because it would have been stupid (and illegal!) to do otherwise. On the continent the situation was different, so my habit changed. But with some habits, like nail-biting or smoking, we wish we didn't do, and we don't understand why we do. If you believe you smoke merely because you got into the habit, it is logical to believe that you can break the habit merely by abstaining for long enough. But you weren't smoking out of habit. What we have to remove is the reason you got into the 'habit' in the first place.

24 February

The second reason the experts give is that it is necessary to endure severe physical withdrawal pains if you try to abstain from nicotine. Again, examine the facts: smokers can sleep all night without a cigarette and don't wake up in physical agony. They are in no physical pain whatsoever.

25 February

Nowadays most smokers leave the bedroom before lighting up. Many will eat breakfast first. Others will wait until they've left the house, and some will even wait until they get to work. Many heavy smokers have no problem with long non-smoking flights. Casual smokers can abstain for days and suffer no physical pain whatsoever. I went overnight from smoking one hundred cigarettes a day to zero and experienced no physical withdrawal pains.

26 February

The torture that smokers suffer when they quit on willpower is purely mental. For reasons they don't understand, they still want a cigarette but won't allow themselves to have one. Little wonder they feel deprived and miserable. It's the same feeling that sends them searching for an all-night garage. That panic feeling reaches its peak when we are actually smoking the last cigarette in the packet. How can that possibly be caused by withdrawal?

27 February

The third reason the experts give to explain why it is difficult to quit is you and your lack of willpower. It takes willpower to quit, they proclaim. If you don't succeed, it's not their fault but yours – you just haven't got what it takes. And what is the valuable advice that these so-called experts give you? That smoking is a filthy, disgusting habit that ruins your health and wealth? Weren't you aware of that already? Isn't that why you sought their help?

28 February

Failing to stop smoking is not due to lack of willpower, but to a conflict of will. I knew I was very strong-willed and couldn't understand why friends who considered themselves weak-willed could successfully quit, but I couldn't. But if you study your smoking acquaintances, you will find that, apart from their smoking, many are both intelligent and strong-willed. The fact that you want to quit proves that you are a reasonably intelligent person. But let's accept the facts: since nobody other than you forces you to smoke, there must be some force that makes you want to continue, otherwise you would already be a non-smoker.

29 February

The odds are that it's not a leap year. If it happens to be one – take the day off. By the way, are you still analyzing your own smoking and that of other smokers? Tomorrow is the beginning of March, the month that comes in like a lion and goes out like a lamb. This March you'll do the opposite – enter it like a lamb and leave it like a lion!

MARCH

1 March

Another common myth is that before the connection between smoking and lung cancer was established, we were not aware that smoking was harmful. Not so. In the First World War cigarettes were referred to as gaspers. Similarly, they were called fags because they fagged you out. The lung cancer threat came as no surprise to me. It was obvious that there was something evil and unnatural about breathing those filthy fumes into my lungs all day, every day.

2 March

Nicotine is a poison widely used in pesticides because of its destructive effect on all living organisms. It is measured in milligrams, as it takes so little to reach a lethal dose. If all the nicotine from one cigarette were extracted and injected into you, it would kill you. Fortunately, when it is smoked, it is delivered in such small doses that it doesn't (or not immediately).

3 March

In the early days of manufacturing, just the leaves and tender stalks of the tobacco plant were harvested, and the nicotine extracted from them. Today's technology means that the whole plant is now leached of its poisonous chemical. The tobacco is then crushed, dried and shredded, and the extract is put back in very precise quantities, along with about 600 other toxic chemicals. The amount of nicotine in each cigarette is carefully calculated to ensure that the body gets just enough to feel the effects of withdrawal once it has almost completed the process of removing the poison from the blood.

4 March

Supposing we believed that there was no danger whatsoever attached to being a grand prix driver, and then some scientist did a study to prove it was a very dangerous pastime. Armed with this knowledge, who would be regarded as weak-willed, the drivers who hadn't the guts to continue their beloved sport, or those who had?

5 March

I'm not trying to justify smoking, merely pointing out that all smokers have this permanent tug-of-war in their minds. Not a lack of willpower, but a conflict of will. When the connection between smoking and lung cancer was made, many smokers found the risks they ran more frightening than life without their friend and helper. I was one of many who believed that life without cigarettes was more frightening than running those risks.

6 March

Although, like all smokers, I felt unclean, weak and stupid for being controlled by a habit that I loathed, whenever I tried to stop, I was utterly miserable. I took what appeared to me to be a very logical decision: I would rather have the shorter, more exciting, life of the smoker than the longer, boring life of the ex-smoker.

7 March

If that were the true choice, I would still be a smoker. Correction. I would already have been dead about 20 years ago. But the difficulty today is trying to imagine how I could have sunk so low as to believe that a smoker's life was more exciting than a non-smoker's, or that a non-smoker's life was more boring than a smoker's.

8 March

Let's explode another of these illusions. It is true that smokers tend to light a cigarette when they are bored. But open your mind. When you smoke a cigarette are you really thinking: this is probably the most exciting and fascinating experience of my life. I light a cigarette then I inhale the filthy, cancerous fumes into my lungs. Gosh! I'm so lucky! Non-smokers never get that pleasure.

9 March

If you've followed my instructions and smoked your cigarettes consciously, you will have learned that smokers don't get that pleasure either. Cigarettes don't relieve boredom; on the contrary they are a major cause of boredom. Can you visualize anything more boring than chain-smoking 100 cigarettes a day for over 30 years?

10 March

So if my claim that smoking provides no genuine pleasure or benefits whatsoever is true, how is it possible that millions of smokers dead and alive have been deluded? As I have stated, the nicotine trap is the most subtle, ingenious confidence trick that Mother Nature and mankind have combined to lay, and I am the first person to see through it.

11 March

Just as an ingenious conjuring trick ceases to appear magical once the trick is explained, so the nicotine trap is simplicity itself once you see through it. You may have noticed that I never refer to the 'smoking trap'. If you've ever tried to switch to herbal cigarettes you will know that, no matter how long you persevere, you will never suffer the illusion of enjoying them.

12 March

If you've tried switching to roll-ups, a pipe or cigars on the basis that because they taste awful it will cut down your intake, you will have discovered that just as your first experimental cigarette tasted foul, but appeared to be enjoyable once you 'acquired' the taste, so you will eventually learn to 'acquire' the taste of any substance that contains nicotine.

13 March

Do you believe heroin addicts inject themselves because they enjoy injections, or to deliver the drug? Do you believe coke addicts sniff cocaine because they enjoy sniffing, or to get the effects of the drug? Do you believe snuff-takers took snuff because they enjoyed sniffing, or because snuff is just dried tobacco and contained nicotine?

14 March

As any fireman or miner will tell you, there is no pleasure in breathing poisonous fumes into your lungs. It's difficult to think of a more ridiculous pastime than doing so on a daily basis and to have to spend a small fortune for the privilege. We start smoking for stupid reasons. The only reason smokers continue to smoke is: BECAUSE THEY ARE ADDICTED TO NICOTINE.

15 March

'Beware the Ides of March!' So if it's not smoking that provides the benefits, is it nicotine? No. There are no benefits, whether you sniff it, inhale it, chew it or absorb it from a patch on your arm.

16 March

Nicotine not only kills insects, it currently kills approximately 5 million people on this planet every year. However, it is the effects of the drug nicotine that create the illusion that we obtain some pleasure or help from smoking. The tobacco plant is indigenous to South America, and is the same genus as deadly nightshade. It is the most addictive drug known to mankind. Just one dose can make you addicted.

17 March

It is commonly believed that nicotine is the disgusting brown stain that smokers have on their fingers and teeth. In fact, the brown stain is caused by the tars. Nicotine itself is a colourless, oily compound. At one time over 90 per cent of the adult male population of western society was addicted to it.

18 March

Every puff on a cigarette delivers, via the lungs and the bloodstream to the brain, a small dose of nicotine that acts more rapidly than a dose of heroin injected directly into a vein. If it takes you 20 puffs to smoke a cigarette, with just one cigarette you take 20 shots of nicotine.

19 March

If you are one of those who believe they do not inhale, you are mistaken. For most of our lives we are not aware that we are breathing, but we'd soon become aware of it if we weren't. In any event, there would be little point in lighting the cigarette if we didn't breathe in the nicotine.

20 March

The first experimental inhalations of nicotine don't even offer the illusion of pleasure or help. Fortunately most smokers remember how foul the experience was and how hard they had to persevere, not to 'acquire' the taste, but to inhale without coughing or feeling sick.

21 March

As with all addictive drugs, it's not so much about the pleasure of taking them, but about the effect the drug has when it begins to leave the body. The so-called experts lead us to believe that we only suffer withdrawal pangs when we try to stop. In fact the only reason anyone continues to smoke is in a vain attempt to relieve the withdrawal syndrome created by the previous dose of nicotine.

22 March

The moment you extinguish a cigarette the nicotine starts to leave your body. This creates an empty, insecure feeling, almost identical to a hunger for food. We only know it as that feeling of needing something to do with our hands or simply as: I want or need a cigarette! Within 30 minutes of extinguishing a cigarette, levels of nicotine in the bloodstream drop by half, and after an hour, by three-quarters. This explains why most smokers get through about 20 cigarettes a day.

23 March

Immediately you light another cigarette the nicotine is replaced and the empty, insecure feeling disappears. This creates a pleasant feeling which smokers describe as enjoyable, satisfying or relaxing. It's rather like removing tight shoes. Youngsters tend to describe it as a 'hit' or a 'buzz'. Why the difference in the description? Because when we are learning to smoke, no way can the experience be described as pleasurable.

24 March

I refer to that empty, insecure feeling as the 'little monster'. Why the 'little monster'? Because although it is a genuine physical irritation, it is so subtle and slight that it's as hardly noticeable. The truth is that 99.99 per cent of smokers have lived and died without even realizing that it exists. For years I described myself as a nicotine addict. I also described myself as a golf addict. In neither case did I believe that I was actually addicted to a drug.

25 March

I thought nicotine was just a filthy, brown substance that stained my fingers and teeth. I certainly never suspected that trying to feed the insatiable appetite of the 'little monster' was the only reason that made me and every other smoker light up.

26 March

Don't worry if at this stage you are having difficulty in accepting this concept. Surely if it were as simple as that, it would be obvious, and Allen Carr wouldn't have been the only one to have worked it out. A clever conjuring trick only becomes obvious once the trick is explained. In the days before Galileo, when you watched the sun rise in the east and set in the west, it merely reinforced what the 'experts' and everyone else on the planet believed: that the sun moved round the earth.

27 March

Today we know that the earth moves round the sun. The illusion was created by one simply explained misconception. But so powerful is that simple illusion that it took mankind over a million years to explode the myth. Even today, we still visualize the sun rising in the east and setting in the west, rather than the earth spinning on its own axis until the sun comes into or goes out of view.

28 March

Before March leaves like a lamb and you leave it like a lion, I need you to understand one fact clearly: non-smokers don't need to poison their bodies in order to enjoy a meal or to answer the phone. Neither did you before you fell into the nicotine trap. And neither will you in future once you've escaped from it.

29 March

The only reason any smoker lights the next cigarette is in the vain attempt to relieve the empty, insecure feeling created by the previous cigarette. Once you can see that each cigarette, far from relieving that feeling, merely creates it, then you will have no more desire to light a cigarette than to place your hands in boiling water just to get the relief of removing them from it.

30 March

No one enjoys unhealthy levels of stress. It causes physical and emotional turmoil. You feel insecure, vulnerable and unable to cope. Chemicals released into the bloodstream create physical reactions to fear and anxiety, and may produce an empty feeling. This feeling is identical to the one you get when you want a cigarette. It's not surprising then that the smoker's brain gets confused and in times of stress will naturally short-circuit to the quickest known 'remedy'.

31 March

You do feel more relaxed, more confident, better able to concentrate and to cope with stress when you light a cigarette. Some smokers therefore argue that the cigarette is providing some genuine benefit. However it is also a fact that when we remove tight shoes we feel more relaxed. But no one would argue that wearing tight shoes is relaxing. It is equally obvious that it's only smokers that get the panic feeling of craving a cigarette. Far from relieving that feeling, each cigarette merely perpetuates it.

APRIL

1 April

The winter of our discontent is passed. Why is spring such an awe-inspiring time? Because every spring we witness the incredible rebirth of nature. This spring will be the most precious of your life. For years you've been living with the depression caused by being a captive of nicotine addiction. You've had an ever-increasing black shadow looming over your life.

2 April

April Fool's Day is now over, and you are going to escape from being one of the biggest of all fools: one who spends hard-earned money to breathe filthy and disgusting cancerous fumes into your lungs in order to try to get back to the state of peace and tranquillity you enjoyed for the whole of your life before you were unfortunate enough to light your first cigarette.

3 April

Can it really be that simple? That the only reason any smoker continues to smoke is a vain attempt to get back to the level of confidence and relaxation they enjoyed the whole of their lives before they were unfortunate enough to light that first cigarette? You might find it difficult to accept this fact, but I assure you that it's as simple as that.

4 April

There are many pathetic aspects to being a nicotine addict, but the most pathetic of all is when smokers are trying to describe to somewhat sceptical non-smokers the actual pleasure they get from smoking. The only pleasure they get is trying to feel like a non-smoker, and ironically the one thing that prevents them from achieving their object is the next cigarette.

5 April

Surely it cannot be that simple. Wouldn't it have been obvious to millions of other people? Don't under-estimate the ingenuity of the trap. There are several reasons why it is very difficult to see through. From birth we've all been subjected to massive brain-washing. Smokers tell us how enjoyable smoking is and how it relaxes them and steadies their nerves. Why shouldn't we believe them? Surely they wouldn't continue to smoke if it weren't true?

6 April

We've also been brainwashed to believe that smoking is a sign of adulthood: that strong men and sophisticated ladies smoke. Little surprise that sooner or later our curiosity has to be satisfied. I don't know how many cats have been killed by curiosity, but I do know that smoking is currently responsible for the early, prolonged and exceedingly painful demise of 5 million smokers per annum.

7 April

Smoking is depicted widely in magazines, on television and in movies. Subtle messages are conveyed by the body language of a smoker shown lighting up on the screen. When you see an angry person, perhaps quarrelling with their boss or their lover, who afterwards lights a cigarette, they visibly relax as they inhale. This is a strong message: cigarettes help in stressful situations.

8 April

Even though many countries now have laws that ban the showing or promoting of smoking on TV or in films, the reality is that it still happens. A 2004 survey shows a 46 per cent increase in the depiction of smoking in Hollywood films. The justification for this is 'artistic licence'. Documents from tobacco companies have shown that it might have more to do with the fact that some high-profile movie stars are prepared to accept money for handling tobacco products in their films.

9 April

The Hollywood screenwriter Joe Eszterhas was responsible for creating a scene in *Basic Instinct* involving Sharon Stone smoking a cigarette. He originally defended his decision to purposely eroticize the scene by claiming 'artistic licence'. Since contracting throat cancer as a direct result of his own smoking, he has become a staunch defender of banning the depiction of smoking on TV and in films. He knows the impact a carefully crafted scene can have on viewers: you need to become aware too.

10 April

The lucky ones find those first cigarettes so horrible that they are never tempted to light another. The unlucky ones persevere and, before they even realize it, they are hooked.

11 April

Of course, at the beginning, we don't buy cigarettes every day, but just when we go out for the evening, relax at weekends or go on holiday. Before we realize it, we are buying and smoking cigarettes every day. In fact, it's not long before we start to feel insecure without a packet of cigarettes around.

12 April

I want you to concentrate on that feeling of insecurity. Did cigarettes really taste so good in those days? Were you really smoking because it made you feel grown-up, strong or sophisticated? Or were you just another of the millions who had been sucked into this sinister trap? You began buying and smoking those cigarettes regularly because the 'little monster' was taking control of your life.

13 April

So having been brainwashed to believe that smoking provides a pleasure and a crutch, once we persevere to 'acquire' the taste, why should we even question this belief when it appears to be true? When nicotine addicts are smoking, they do actually feel better able to concentrate, more relaxed and confident, and less nervous, bored or distressed than when they are not smoking. We don't understand how a cigarette achieves all these contradictory effects. So what? Why even question it so long as it does?

14 April

In fact we only begin to question it once the accumulated effects of smoking begin to affect our health, energy and finances. The reason all drug addiction is difficult to see through is because it works back to front: only when the drug is leaving our body do we suffer the empty, insecure feeling. Since we are not smoking at that time and because there is no physical pain and the feeling is so imperceptible, we don't blame it on the previous cigarette. The moment we light up, the nicotine is replaced and we feel more confident and relaxed. So we attribute magical properties to the cigarette.

15 April

The final reason that it is difficult to see through the trap is exactly because the feeling is so imperceptible. There is no physical pain, in fact we only know the feeling as: 'I want/need a cigarette!' In order to understand nicotine addiction completely, you need to understand hunger.

16 April

We think of hunger as a somewhat unpleasant experience. But imagine you are the creator and have created this incredible variety of species on the planet. How would you ensure that they didn't all die of starvation? You could personally feed each one of them daily. But that would be a tremendous hassle. So why not do as the creator did: invent this ingenious device called hunger.

17 April

What actually happens when you feel hungry? Are you doubled up with physical pain? Your stomach might be rumbling, but that isn't physical pain. Isn't it true that we only know hunger as an empty, insecure feeling of: 'I need to eat.'

18 April

Many people believe that the real pleasure in eating is the taste of good food. Not so. It is not just coincidence that the French wish you 'bon appetit' before a meal, rather than 'bonne nourriture' (good food). The real pleasure in eating is to satisfy the empty, insecure feeling we know as hunger.

19 April

It is true that we would rather satisfy our hunger with some foods than others – just as we would rather satisfy our craving for nicotine with certain brands of cigarettes than others. But just as some starving people have been reduced to cannibalism to avoid starvation, so smokers will smoke old rope rather than nothing if they can't get their favourite brand.

20 April

So, although there is no physical pain, don't underestimate the effect of this empty, insecure feeling. If it can drive God-fearing people to cannibalism and if smokers would rather have limbs removed than quit smoking, it is real! The empty feeling created by a craving for nicotine is identical to a hunger for food. However, one will not satisfy the other.

21 April

It is this similarity between satisfying a hunger for food and satisfying a craving for nicotine that fools us into believing that we get some genuine pleasure and/or crutch from smoking. In fact they are complete opposites.

22 April

Satisfying a hunger for food is a genuinely enjoyable experience, whereas breathing foul and cancerous fumes into your lungs can hardly be described as pleasant. Food is essential to our survival, and to supply us with energy and to keep us fit and healthy. Nicotine is a powerful poison that makes us lethargic and shortens our lives. Food doesn't create hunger, but genuinely satisfies it, and it enables us to enjoy three meals a day throughout our lives. Smoking creates a craving for nicotine and is the one thing that won't satisfy it.

23 April

It wouldn't be so bad if, when you lit a cigarette, you did get back to feeling as good as you did before you lit the first one. Unfortunately, even when you are smoking that cigarette, you still feel more nervous and less relaxed than if you had never lit that first cigarette. Why? Immunity.

24 April

The human body is a very sophisticated survival machine. Whether we like it or not, our instinct is to ensure that we survive. We think of fear as a weakness. On the contrary, we should remember it is like a fire alarm, warning us of danger and telling us to remove the threat.

25 April

The foul taste, the coughing fit and the feeling of nausea when we light those first cigarettes act as an alarm signal. Through them the body is saying: 'You are feeding me poison! Please stop!' When we continue to smoke, our bodies assume we do so because we have no choice. The body doesn't think it's because we are incredibly stupid.

26 April

Miraculously the body then tries to help us out, by building an immunity to that poison. Rasputin built up such an immunity to arsenic that he could survive 20 times the dose that would kill a normal person. However, immunity is a two-edged sword.

27 April

Just as the body builds an immunity to the poisonous effects of nicotine, so each time you light up, you only partially relieve the empty, insecure feeling. Therefore, even while you are smoking a cigarette, you still feel more nervous and less relaxed than a non-smoker.

28 April

You might expect smokers to recognize this situation. However, as is the case with all drug addiction, the more the drug drags you down, the greater your illusion that the drug is helping you. An alcoholic said to his friend: 'If you had my problems, you'd drink as much as I do.' The friend replied: 'If I drank as much as you do, I would have your problems!'

29 April

The nature of all drug addiction is that non-smokers, non-heroin addicts and non-alcoholics can see clearly that not only does the drug provide no benefits whatsoever, but that it is the major cause of the problems the addict is trying to escape from by taking the drug. And, like all drugs, the more it ruins your life and drags you down, the more dependent you feel on the illusory crutch.

30 April

The myth that smoking benefits the smoker is a big one in the canon of smoker's lore, but it's a pygmy in comparison with the notion that it is difficult to stop smoking. I don't dispute that most smokers find it difficult, if not impossible, to do just that. But it doesn't have to be so.

I May

What better time than May to discover why smokers find it difficult to quit with other methods? Better still – to discover just how easy and enjoyable it is to escape from the nicotine trap with this method. However, before proceeding, we need to recap.

2 May

If you have opened your mind and understood everything I've said so far, you will not only realize that smoking doesn't provide any benefits whatsoever, but also that the 'little monster' actually creates the empty, insecure feeling. Smoking doesn't aid concentration, but, like any other aggravation, such as a persistent and irritating noise, you can't concentrate until the distraction has been removed.

3 May

You arrive home from work. You feel sweaty, dirty, thirsty, hungry and tired. So you take a shower, change your clothes, have a drink, eat your evening meal and relax on the sofa to watch the TV. If you are addicted to nicotine, you won't feel completely satisfied until you light up and feed the 'little monster'. Only now do you feel completely relaxed.

4 May

But all you have really done is to remove a series of aggravations that were preventing you from feeling completely relaxed. The shower and change of clothing removed the sweaty, dirty feeling, the drink removed your thirst and the food satisfied your hunger. Isn't it obvious? Breathing poisonous fumes into your lungs cannot relax you. You only do it to satisfy that empty, insecure feeling of wanting or needing a cigarette.

5 May

Get it very clear in your mind that each cigarette, far from satisfying that empty, insecure feeling, actually causes it. This is why there is a chain reaction to addictive drugs. I love the taste of lobster, but I have never reached the stage where I get into a panic unless I have 20 lobsters hanging round my neck. In fact, it wouldn't bother me if I never have another lobster in my life. I hated the taste of cigarettes, but the mere thought of being without them created a feeling of panic.

6 May

It should be good news to learn that smoking provides you with no pleasures or benefits whatsoever. But if you've already gone through the misery of trying to stop using a willpower method, this news may be of little comfort. You might even be tempted to abandon your attempt.

7 May

Please don't fall into that trap. The most ingenious aspect of all drug addiction is that the lower it knocks you down, the greater the fear of being without it. Why do you think stopping smoking is by far the most popular New Year resolution? If you really want to do something you don't put it off. But smokers who say they are going to quit do. They can't bring themselves to stop today so they pretend to themselves, and everyone else, that they'll stop tomorrow – even though they've probably made the same promise several years in a row.

8 May

Allow me to reassure you that you have absolutely nothing to lose. If only I could show smokers how fantastic they would feel just three weeks after they'd extinguished their final cigarette. I don't just mean health- and energy-wise, but also in terms of confidence and freedom. Unfortunately I can't do that. But you can do it for yourself! Just use your common sense and imagination.

9 May

Now we can get down to explaining why smokers find it so difficult to quit when using a 'willpower' method. From birth we've been brainwashed into believing that smoking genuinely achieves all these magical benefits. Once we fall into the trap, the addiction seems to confirm the illusions of the brainwashing.

10 May

At the same time, as our daily intake gradually increases and the cumulative effects of our smoking increasingly damage both our health and our finances, it begins to dawn on us that we too have fallen into the trap, and that it's about time to escape. But the trap is so designed that we put off the evil day for as long as possible.

11 May

In addition, it's impossible to ignore the whingeing stoppers: those ex-smokers who describe in vivid detail the months of misery they had to endure, and how they have abstained for years but continually remind you how much they enjoyed smoking and how they could still 'murder' for a cigarette.

12 May

It is these whingeing ex-smokers who seem to confirm the terrifying idea: 'Once a smoker, always a smoker!' Just as some people try to divide the world into black and white, Protestant and Catholic, rich and poor, and so on, I once divided the world into smokers and non-smokers. Non-smokers were insipid, lack-lustre people who were so frightened of life that they would be happier living inside a sterilized plastic bag.

13 May

It wasn't until after I'd finally escaped from the nicotine trap that I realized that most of my friends were ex-smokers and that several of them had never been smokers. Such is the fear and distortion of perception caused by drug addiction.

14 May

So, when we finally pluck up enough courage to make a serious attempt to quit, we are convinced it will be difficult and that we'll have to use immense willpower. We've also been brainwashed into believing that we have to go through an indeterminate period of deprivation and misery during which we'll continue to crave cigarettes, but no longer be allowed to satisfy that craving.

15 May

But above all we believe that we are 'giving up' a genuine pleasure and/or crutch! Doesn't 'giving up' imply a genuine sacrifice? We don't give up cancer or any other disease. We get cured of diseases. We don't give up an addiction – we escape from it!

16 May

Little wonder that with a 'willpower' method of quitting, we start off with a feeling of doom and gloom and impending failure. Even so, we know we didn't need to smoke before we fell into the trap. We also know that smoking is seriously affecting our health and wealth. Only completely insensitive or selfish smokers can close their minds to the consternation they cause their families.

17 May

So we start off determined, knowing that smoking is a mug's game. In our minds, we build up all the valid reasons why we'll be better off as non-smokers, and they all sound completely logical. But then something completely illogical happens: the 'little monster' hasn't been fed. We only know that feeling as: 'I want a cigarette.' Because we believe we've made a genuine sacrifice, we start to crave a cigarette.

18 May

But we won't allow ourselves to have a cigarette. We believe that a cigarette will satisfy the craving, so we feel deprived and miserable. What do smokers do when they feel deprived and miserable? Of course they light a cigarette. But now we won't allow ourselves to smoke a cigarette, so we just feel more miserable. It's a cause and effect situation. The more miserable we feel – the greater the need to end that misery. Eventually our willpower runs out and we light up.

19 May

I used to bang my head against the wall, hoping that my wife, or one of my children would say, 'I can't bear to watch you go through this misery! Please have a cigarette!' This was the excuse I'd been waiting for. I was in no physical pain, but I wanted to give in. I was hoping to make the excuse that I was giving in not because I was weak-willed, but to avoid the irritation I was causing my family.

20 May

Hence the illusion is created that smokers suffer terrible physical nicotine withdrawal pains when they try to quit. I'm not belittling the misery smokers go through at such time, but it's mental not physical. One of the great advantages of Easyway is that we remove the mental anguish before we extinguish the final cigarette.

21 May

Most 'willpower' attempts at quitting end in a compromise, such as, 'I can't face life without cigarettes completely, so I'll cut down to five a day,' or, 'From now on I'll only smoke cigarettes on special occasions.' Cutting down sounds logical, but let me explain why it cannot work.

22 May

Because we are all casual smokers when we start smoking and seemed quite happy to be so, we believe that we simply get into the 'habit' of smoking too many. We think that if we can reverse the process and discipline ourselves to smoke only five cigarettes a day, we will soon get into the habit of only wanting or needing five a day. It sounds logical, but it doesn't work.

23 May

We didn't smoke out of habit, but to feed the 'little monster'. As with all addictive drugs, as our bodies become immune to it, we need to smoke more and more, not less and less, as time goes on. Imagine the 'little monster' as an imperceptible itch. The natural inclination is to scratch it.

24 May

If you ask a smoker, 'Do you need a cigarette?' they will often reply, 'I don't *need* one, but I would like one.' To them the distinction is important. 'Need' implies addiction. 'Want' or 'would like' suggests they are in control. In fact, need and want are the same. If you have an itch, you feel a need to scratch it. This need makes you want to scratch it.

25 May

You must have wondered why some smokers seem contented to smoke just five a day, and others (like the smoker I was) need to chain-smoke. It was always a puzzle to me. In fact the answer is very simple. It's the perpetual tug-of-war that all smokers suffer from. Half our brain is saying, 'This filthy habit is killing me and costing me a fortune.' But the other half is saying, 'But I need a cigarette!'

26 May

Some people can't afford to smoke as much as they'd like to. Others limit their intake because their lungs can't physically cope with the poison, or they are terrified that they will get lung cancer, emphysema or heart disease if they smoke too much. Isn't another reason that 'giving up' is the favourite New Year resolution because over the Christmas and New Year celebrations, even casual smokers wake up with a throat resembling a dried-up riverbed?

27 May

All heavy smokers envy casual smokers. At our clinics when a smoker declares that they only smoke two cigarettes a day, or only smoke on social occasions, the other smokers stare at them in disbelief. Invariably one of them will say something like, 'Why on earth do you want to quit? My dream is to need only two cigarettes a day!'

28 May

If you have been following my instructions, and have opened your mind and studied not only your own smoking but also that of others, it will already have begun to dawn on you that there is no such thing as a happy smoker.

29 May

It's understandable that a chain-smoker like me would discourage his children from falling into the trap. But why do apparently happy casual smokers not encourage their children and grandchildren to share the immense pleasures of smoking? After all, the risk and cost of smoking only two a day are negligible. And indeed, why do such smokers seek help at my clinics?

30 May

Another essential fact to get into your mind is that all smokers are liars. We can be honest, upright citizens in other ways, but with smoking we have to lie. We know that it's a dangerous, expensive and filthy pastime. We also sense that we've fallen into a trap that we don't know how to escape from.

31 May

If every time you lit a cigarette you had to be aware that you were filling your lungs with filthy, disgusting fumes, that this cigarette might just be the one to trigger lung cancer, and that the average 20-a-day smoker spends £50,000 in their lifetime, do you think you would even have the illusion of enjoying that cigarette? So we block our minds to those facts. And because we feel stupid and weak for being smokers, in order to retain some level of self-respect and respect for ourselves and from others, we invent feeble excuses to justify our smoking. Excuses that can easily be seen through by a four-year-old child!

JUNE

1 June

So why do casual smokers want to quit? Observe casual smokers at social occasions. They'll tell you how lucky they are that they only need to smoke five a day. But many will be chain-smoking like every other smoker at the party.

2 June

So if smoking is such a pleasure and a help, why is it that smokers always boast about how little they smoke? If I were to say to you: 'Do you know, I can go a whole week without eating peas and it doesn't bother me in the slightest.' What would I actually be telling you: that I have no problem with peas? If this is the case, why on earth would I make such a statement?

3 June

When a smoker says, 'I can go a whole week without a cigarette and it doesn't bother me in the slightest', they are trying to convince not just you, but themselves. If it doesn't bother them in the slightest, why do they bother to say so? Could it be to feel superior? No, it's because they are worried about their smoking and trying to justify it. And they have good reason to feel proud of themselves – it's some feat for a nicotine addict to resist scratching the itch for a whole week!

4 June

But if they managed a whole week and it didn't bother them, why did they feel the need to light up at the end of the week? I mean, either you enjoy a cigarette or you don't. If you enjoy a cigarette and your smoking doesn't bother you, why would you want to deprive yourself of that pleasure for a whole week? Once you begin to probe them, the excuses of casual smokers are just as illogical as those of heavy smokers.

5 June

The fact is that casual smokers are more hooked and more miserable than heavy smokers. Hard to believe, but true. The only pleasure any smoker gets when they light up is in scratching the itch. If you are able to light up whenever you become aware that you need or want a cigarette, you can immediately relieve the itch. The effect is identical to immediately relieving a hunger for food.

6 June

But supposing you are hungry and the delicious aroma of your favourite dish is coming from the kitchen. Then there's a power cut and the meal won't be ready for hours. You're in no physical pain. Your stomach might be rumbling but that isn't physical pain. Nevertheless, the intervening period could be described as torture, and won't that dish taste twice as good when you can finally satisfy your hunger?

7 June

This is what happens to smokers who, for whatever reason, discipline themselves not to light up the moment the 'little monster' demands to be fed. At least when you light up whenever you feel the need, although the 'little monster' is controlling your life, the effect is not so bad. But if you won't allow yourself to scratch the itch immediately, you will be spending your whole life just waiting for your next fix.

8 June

The more we smoke, the more it damages our health and pocket and the greater our desire to quit. The illusion of pleasure is created by trying to satisfy the 'little monster'. If we delay scratching the itch, that illusion is greatly increased. So the less we smoke, the more we reduce our desire to quit, and the greater the illusion of pleasure.

9 June

When parents advise their children to 'Quit while you can' it has little effect. Their intake is fairly low at this stage. Both physically and financially, their smoking is creating no problem, and they are convinced, as all smokers once were, that if smoking began to affect their health, they would quit.

10 June

Eventually all drug addicts arrive at what I call 'the critical point'. This is the stage when the cumulative effect smoking has had on our health and pocket obviously outweighs the illusory benefits we are receiving. So we decide to cut down. Remember the nature of all addictive drugs is to crave more and more, not less. At the very time one part of your body and brain needs to increase the intake, another part is saying, 'No, smoke less!' It's an awful dichotomy. From this point on smokers are miserable when they aren't allowed to smoke and miserable when they are.

11 June

Can you imagine how precious a meal would be if you only ate once a day? Can you imagine how much greater the illusion of pleasure would be if you only allowed yourself to smoke one cigarette a day? If the prospect still seems enjoyable to you, bear in mind that the only pleasure a smoker gets from smoking is the ending of the miserable craving.

12 June

This is why casual smokers are more hooked than heavy smokers. The less they smoke, the less it injures their health and finances and, accordingly, the less their desire to quit. The longer they crave, the greater the illusion that smoking creates a crutch or gives pleasure, and the less their desire to quit.

13 June

The nature of all drug addiction is to want to consume more and more rather than less and less. In order to cut down successfully, you would have to exercise willpower and discipline for the rest of your life. If you haven't got sufficient willpower to quit, where on earth are you going to get the willpower to cut down for the rest of your life?

14 June

Fortunately, with Easyway you don't need willpower to quit. But supposing I could arrange it so that you only needed to smoke one cigarette a year. Would you be happy with that situation? If you enjoyed smoking a cigarette, would you really want to wait a whole year to satisfy the craving? If you didn't enjoy a cigarette, why on earth would you want to smoke it?

15 June

I hope the penny is beginning to drop. Once your life has been dominated by nicotine, the prospect of never being allowed to smoke another cigarette can be quite frightening. But does a life of never being allowed to inject yourself with heroin frighten you? Or the prospect of never being allowed to drink another bottle of meths down Skid Row? Of course not. But this is the effect that heroin and alcohol have on those who become addicted to them.

16 June

People in abusive relationships behave very like this. They might hate their abuser but fear of the unknown, of something else, is so great that it prevents them from moving on. Fear creates doubt, paralyzes our capacity for reasoning. Before you became a smoker you did not have this fear. You can blame cigarettes for creating it. When you become a non-smoker, this fear disappears. It is the physical addiction that triggers the ideas — or brainwashing about smoking.

17 June

What is the real difference between a smoker and a non-smoker? That one smokes and the other doesn't? No! This is where smokers who use a willpower method go wrong – they try not to smoke any more. Some actually succeed. I can only admire their willpower.

18 June

However, far from envying them, I have nothing but pity for them. I can't think of anything worse than spending the rest of your life believing you are being deprived of a great pleasure and having to resist temptation. The real difference between smokers and non-smokers is that non-smokers have no more desire to breathe cancerous fumes into their lungs than to inject heroin into their veins.

19 June

If you see just one cigarette as some sort of pleasure or crutch, you will see a million cigarettes in the same way. You are left with just two choices: either to spend the rest of your life in a vain attempt to resist falling for the temptation, or to remain in the nicotine trap until you become just another statistic.

20 June

Fortunately you have a third choice. That is, to remove all the brainwashing and to see smoking as you did before you fell into the trap. So that when you extinguish your final cigarette, it's not with a feeling of fear, trepidation or deprivation – 'I can't/mustn't ever have another cigarette' – but instead, with a feeling of relief, achievement, excitement and elation: 'Isn't it marvellous! I've finally escaped from the nicotine trap! Never again do I need to spend my hard-earned money just for the privilege of inhaling these disgusting fumes into my lungs!'

21 June

So what is it about Easyway that makes it not only easy but enjoyable to quit?

It is easy and enjoyable to quit! Easyway simply removes the illusions that make it difficult. With a 'willpower' method we extinguish what we hope will be our final cigarette and also hope, that provided we have sufficient willpower, we can abstain long enough for the craving to go.

22 June

But why should it go? If you believe that smoking aids concentration and relaxation, and relieves boredom, stress and nervousness, why should you cease to believe that just because you've quit and hope you will never smoke again? If you are convinced that you'll find it difficult to quit, you probably will! If you start off with a feeling of doom and gloom, why should it not continue? After all, absence makes the heart grow fonder.

23 June

If you stop smoking using willpower you force yourself into a self-imposed tantrum like a child being deprived of its chocolates. The stronger-willed that child is, the more it wants the chocolates.

24 June

You might argue that you'll soon be feeling healthier, and have more energy and money. True. But all that does is to remove the reasons that made you want to quit in the first place. If you still believe a cigarette improves a meal or relieves stress, you become vulnerable to thinking: 'Surely an occasional cigarette can't do any harm.'

25 June

Eventually you feel secure enough to try one, just to see what it tastes like, and its taste will range from weird to foul, just as those first cigarettes did. You think, 'How on earth did I get hooked on these filthy things?' Now you feel very secure. But some weeks later, you're out with smoking friends. For some peculiar reason you find yourself wanting another cigarette. You think, 'Where's the harm? I had one three weeks ago and didn't get hooked again then.'

26 June

Little do you realize it, but you are already hooked again. You've fallen back into the identical trap that you fell for as a youngster. The drug will catch you again and it will all happen so slowly and gradually you won't even realize it. Soon you'll be smoking at the same level as when you 'gave up' and making the same excuses not to quit today but tomorrow.

27 June

Many ex-smokers who get hooked again had been contented ex-smokers for many years. Perhaps you are one of them. It may be a consolation for you to know that I never met one who didn't regret starting smoking again. And when I ask them why they started again, their reply is invariably, 'I was a fool!' Don't ever envy smokers – pity them.

28 June

The point is that if you believe there is some genuine pleasure or crutch in smoking, you will be vulnerable for the rest of your life. It is difficult to convince a nervous person that smoking causes, rather than relieves, nervousness. If smoking genuinely relieved nerves, smokers would be more relaxed than non-smokers.

29 June

To sum up the 'willpower' method: with a feeling of doom and gloom, we extinguish what we hope will be our final cigarette, also hoping that, if we have sufficient willpower to endure the misery long enough, we'll wake up one morning shouting, 'Eureka! I've kicked it!'

30 June

But it's absurd to say, 'One day I never want to smoke again' and then to spend the next few days, and possibly the rest of your life, thinking, 'I'd love a cigarette!' I'm not suggesting that smokers are stupid, but the ingenuity of the trap makes us act in an absurd way.

Meanwhile, congratulations. You are now half-way through the course. From now on you've no need either to feel stupid or act absurdly.

JULY

1 July

When you make an attempt to 'give up' using a 'willpower' method, you know no more about the nicotine trap than you did before you tried. In particular, you are not even aware of the existence of the 'little monster'.

2 July

This can be very confusing. You've been building up in your mind all the genuinely powerful arguments against being a smoker. You've probably also wondered what great pleasure there is in breathing filthy fumes into your lungs. And no sooner have you extinguished your final cigarette than you get the feeling, 'I need/want a cigarette.' Because you are not even aware of the existence of the 'little monster', and because you know that a cigarette will relieve this unpleasant feeling, you start craving one.

3 July

Why would anyone crave a cigarette unless they got some genuine help or pleasure from it? Why indeed? So, far from removing the illusion that smoking relieves stress and aids relaxation, a 'willpower' attempt to quit merely reinforces it.

4 July

If you need to concentrate in your job, you will find it impossible when part of your brain wants to smoke and the other half won't allow it to, particularly if you believe that smoking aids concentration. The 'willpower' attempt therefore reinforces the illusion that smoking aids concentration.

5 July

The belief that I couldn't function or concentrate without a cigarette was the main reason I failed when using 'willpower' methods. Even when I understood the nicotine trap and realized that, far from aiding concentration, smoking impeded it, it wasn't until my colleague Robin Hayley put the fallacy in its true perspective that the stupidity of my belief sunk in.

6 July

He said, 'Allen, imagine going to an interview and being told: "This job involves a high level of concentration. It is an accepted fact that smoking aids concentration. So although you are a non-smoker, we would require you to smoke. Only during periods of intense concentration, you understand!" The concept is ludicrous.'

7 July

Nowadays I hate visits to the dentist and medical examinations. It's hard for me to remember that I actually used to enjoy those regular medicals at school. I was a physical fitness fanatic in those days. My attitude was, 'Search as hard as you like, you'll find nothing wrong with this body.' Now you could put that down to the fact that the young feel indestructible. And that's just the point. I did feel indestructible.

8 July

Can it be coincidence that the feeling of indestructibility ended when I fell into the nicotine trap? Let's assume it's Monday morning, you've had pains in your chest and your GP has arranged for an examination at the local hospital. Whether you're a smoker or a non-smoker, you would wake up with a feeling of apprehension. If you're a smoker, that feeling would be increased for two reasons. One, that you've failed to heed all the warnings and you fear the pain is the big C. Two, you've gone eight hours without nicotine and the 'little monster' is crying out to be fed.

9 July

When smokers feel nervous or under stress, the natural tendency is to light a cigarette, and when you light that cigarette, you will feel less nervous than a moment before. This reinforces the illusion that smoking helps to relieve stress. But would you now be laughing and happy — actually looking forward to that visit to the hospital? Of course not! Even while you're smoking that cigarette, you would still be more apprehensive than the non-smoker. And with very good reason.

10 July

Also bear in mind that while you're in the hospital, you won't be allowed to smoke, and would therefore have to suffer the empty, insecure feeling caused by the 'little monster'. It never seems to occur to smokers that at some of the most stressful periods in their lives, like visits to dentists and doctors, they aren't allowed to relieve their withdrawal pangs.

11 July

Because smokers are unable to distinguish the empty, insecure feeling created by the 'little monster' from a hunger for food or from a feeling of insecurity created by normal stress, even after the 'little monster' has long since died, ex-smokers still associate suffering from normal hunger or genuine stress with lighting a cigarette. This highlights another reason why a 'willpower' method makes it virtually impossible to quit.

12 July

How do you know when you have succeeded in 'giving up' smoking? If you decide that your objective is to 'give up' for a whole year, it is obvious that you cannot claim to have achieved your objective until you have abstained for one whole year.

13 July

Doesn't it follow that if your object is to 'give up' permanently, you can't possibly be certain that you've been successful until you reach the end of your life? Even then you won't be aware of, or get any pleasure from, your achievement. Once you're dead, no one phones you on the mobile saying, 'Congratulations! You've actually escaped from the nicotine trap!'

14 July

So, I repeat my question. How do smokers, using a 'willpower 'method, know that they have escaped from the nicotine trap? I suspect that they never do. I don't deny that millions of smokers have gone through the misery of the 'willpower' method and never smoked again. But millions of others were equally convinced, yet did get hooked again.

15 July

But consider the question: when do you know for certain that you have succeeded? Some so-called scientific experts will tell you that it is when you have abstained for a whole year. What could be more unscientific than picking a purely random period without offering a sound reason to justify it? Particularly when you consider that ex-smokers who haven't smoked for over ten years consult our clinics because they are still fighting temptation.

16 July

Is it when you can enjoy a social function, or answer the phone without craving a cigarette, that you can be sure you have succeeded? But how do you know you won't crave one the following week, month or year? My point is that when you achieve something positive, like passing a driving test, you know you've achieved your objective, and you can celebrate.

17 July

But how can you ever know when you've achieved something negative, like never smoking again? Aren't you just spending the rest of your life waiting to see whether you ever smoke again? Or to put it another way: you spend the rest of your life waiting for nothing to happen.

18 July

Perhaps you feel that exactly the same problem will apply with Easyway. I promise you that if you open your mind and follow the instructions it will not. Easyway is the complete opposite. Instead of extinguishing what we hope will be the final cigarette and then forcing ourselves into a tantrum, we first remove the brainwashing. We explain exactly how the confidence trick works.

19 July

Intelligent people fall for confidence tricks, but once you can see through any confidence trick, even a simpleton won't continue to fall for it. Once you realize that there is absolutely nothing to 'give up', that far from smoking relaxing you, relieving stress and boredom, steadying your nerves and aiding concentration, it does the complete opposite, you'll have no more desire to light a cigarette than to inject yourself with heroin.

20 July

With Easyway, we remove all the brainwashing first. When you extinguish that final cigarette, you know that you are 'giving up' absolutely nothing, and are achieving a marvellous escape from the Number 1 killer disease in western society. Far from a feeling of doom and gloom, there is a relief and exaltation that you no longer need to live in this nightmare of spending a fortune to destroy your health, just because you're a slave to this insidious drug.

21 July

Let me make it quite clear, nicotine is the most powerful addictive drug known to mankind. Why else would over 90 per cent of adult males in western society have at one time been smokers? You have to look beyond the drug itself to find an answer to this question.

22 July

With any drug, be it heroin, cocaine, alcohol or nicotine, what makes you an addict is not the chemical influence of the drug, but the belief that you get some genuine benefit from it – or, more accurately, that you can't enjoy or cope with life without it. The chemical effect creates the illusion, but like any confidence trick, once you see through it, it ceases to be a confidence trick.

23 July

Heroin addicts can only withstand the punishment their daily doses of poison inflict upon them for 10–15 years before their bodies start to break down. It can take as long as 50 or 60 years for a smoker's body to break down. It's so slow we barely notice until it's too late.

24 July

Some smokers begin to panic when I tell them that smoking isn't habit but addiction to nicotine. They think, 'If habits are difficult to break, how much more difficult is it going to be if I'm also addicted to the most powerful drug known to mankind?' I cannot emphasize this too often: it is not only easy, but can actually be enjoyable to quit if you follow all the instructions.

25 July

Another great difficulty with a 'willpower' method is the void that 'giving up' tends to leave in our lives. We are not only brainwashed to believe that a cigarette provides several contradictory benefits, but we are also brainwashed to believe that we cannot enjoy life or cope with stress without help.

26 July

For other creatures on the planet, giving birth is a completely natural function. But in western society, not only does the birth itself usually mean a stay in hospital, but both mother and baby are subjected to months of pre- and post-natal attention.

27 July

I'm not criticizing this procedure, but merely pointing out that it creates the impression that mother and baby are weak and vulnerable creatures. The fact that the whole procedure often involves the administration of drugs and food and vitamin supplements merely serves to exacerbate the feeling.

28 July

Whereas a giraffe, for example, can stand, walk and run just a few hours after birth, a child takes at least six months. It will then be mollycoddled for the first few years of its life. The slightest cough or rash will provoke a visit to the doctor and result in pills, ointments or other medicines being prescribed. The child will also receive injections for several diseases it would probably never get in any case.

29 July

I emphasize that I'm not knocking the system. Or even suggesting that it should be changed, but merely pointing out that this 'Don't go out in the rain without your mac or you'll get pneumonia' attitude doesn't exactly encourage a feeling of indestructibility. Even as adults we need a whole range of cosmetics and toiletries to help us cope with the effects of natural life, such as going out in the sun.

30 July

We have been brainwashed to feel like physical weaklings, compared to wild animals like elephants and tigers. We are not! Our bodies are made up of the same type of flesh and bones. In fact, elephants and tigers are in danger of extinction. With the advantage of our superior brains, we have colonized every corner of the planet.

31 July

So strong and successful is the human race, that the main threat to the survival of the planet – and all species on it – is over-population and pollution. I once believed my feeling of indestructibility was due to ignorance of the young. Now I know better.

AUGUST

1 August

My father was a chain-smoker. In my early twenties, I was shocked to hear him say that he had no wish to live until 50. At 48, with my permanent smoker's cough and frequent bouts of asthma and bronchitis, I knew I wouldn't survive to see 50 unless I quit smoking.

2 August

Possibly you are thinking, 'No wonder he quit, I would also if my smoking had got to that stage!' But the point was that I didn't quit! I was actually prepared to die rather than stop smoking. It wasn't that I wanted to die, I just thought, 'If this is the quality of my life with my pleasure and crutch, would life be worth living without it?'

3 August

I can only assume my father had reached the same conclusion. He was unlucky, although he did survive to his early fifties. I was very, very lucky. I discovered Easyway. Non-addicts can see clearly that the addict is getting no benefit or crutch whatsoever from smoking, and that in fact the drug is the main cause of the problems for which they are taking it. Many of the insights I'm revealing to you now I couldn't see until I escaped from the nicotine prison.

4 August

I remember as a child having a great fear of dying, not of the process, but of being dead. This was because I had a great joy in living. The true reason that I was prepared to die rather than 'give up' smoking was that I had lost the joy of living.

5 August

Another ingenious and insidious aspect of all addictive drugs is that the process of dragging you down happens so gradually that you are not aware of it. It's rather like growing old: the face you see in the mirror each day appears identical to the one you saw yesterday. Not until we examine a photo taken years earlier does the ageing process become apparent. Even then we tend to sweeten the pill, by saying, 'Didn't I look young' rather than, 'Don't I look old!'

6 August

I'd heard of other smokers who woke up one morning and by some unexplained miracle just never wanted to smoke any more. I believed that if that ever happened to me, by far the biggest benefit would be to my health.

7 August

Perhaps you've been hoping that someday a similar miracle will happen to you. If so, don't waste your time. I've already warned you that all drug addicts are notorious liars. I've probed these stories and I promise you there is always more to it.

8 August

Often the smoker has had a health scare or has visited a close friend dying of lung cancer. The experience shocks the smoker into opening his eyes. He thinks, 'That could easily be me lying there.' It would be better to say something like, 'I decided to quit and that's the sort of person I am. Once I make up my mind to do something, there's no stopping me!' Rather than, 'I quit because I was terrified!'

9 August

Perhaps you are wondering if that's what eventually happened to me. No. I was prepared to die, not out of bravery, but because I thought it was impossible for me to quit. What happened to me seemed like a miracle, but far from being inexplicable, I knew exactly why I would never smoke again.

10 August

Incredibly, not only was improved health not the main gain from quitting, it wasn't even close. It's true that the permanent smoker's cough disappeared after just a few days, and the asthma and bronchitis attacks disappeared completely. But the main problem wasn't the attacks themselves — I could cope with those — it was the embarrassment of having a coughing fit in front of non-smokers. Most were too polite to comment, but they were obviously thinking, 'What sort of an imbecile is he?'

11 August

Such is the fear of being without our little friend and crutch, that we block our minds to the sheer slavery of being a smoker. I remember as a child being told the story of a miserable man with a genie sitting on his shoulders, its legs almost choking him, dictating his whole life. Isn't being dominated by nicotine very similar?

12 August

We can't enjoy a meal without a cigarette. We can't answer the phone without a cigarette. The thought of going on holiday and not being able to obtain our favourite brand fills us with dread! That panic feeling when we are running low. Will the next person we meet be one of those high and mighty non-smokers? If I light up here, will someone complain?

Non-smokers don't have these problems. I cannot tell you how wonderful it is not to have to worry whether you can or can't smoke – not to have your life dominated by this evil weed.

13 August

Even though we try to block our minds to the effect smoking has on our health, our pocket and our self-respect, we sense that we've fallen into a trap and it's like an ever-increasing black shadow hanging over our lives. I cannot over-emphasize the relief and joy of being rid of the genie and black shadow.

14 August

I was convinced that smoking gave me confidence and courage. Many smokers can't make a phone call without lighting up. I'd reached the stage where I couldn't even change a TV channel without lighting up! What's so stressful about making a phone call, let alone changing a TV channel? Non-smokers don't have this problem. Why wasn't it obvious to me that far from giving me courage and confidence, nicotine was destroying them?

15 August

The second greatest benefit of escaping from the nicotine trap was energy. Sadly, it is true that we take good health for granted. Only when we have been incapacitated by an accident, or fall ill, do we appreciate fully how nice it is to feel healthy.

16 August

For years I couldn't distinguish the difference between not feeling ill and feeling great to be alive. That's because for most of my life I wasn't feeling ill. But I'd forgotten completely what it was like to feel great. I used to struggle to get out of bed in the morning and never felt completely awake. After the evening meal, I would fall asleep watching TV. I put it down to old age.

17 August

Shortly after quitting, I started to wake up over an hour earlier feeling as if I'd had a great night's sleep. I began to experience a feeling that I hadn't felt since my early twenties. Even though I was at least two stones over the recommended weight of a man of my height, I had energy! For years I'd known that I needed to exercise. Now I actually wanted to. I lost two stones in six months.

18 August

The ending of the coughing fits, asthma and bronchitis was great. So was the ending of the slavery – not having my life controlled by an evil that I loathed? The removal of the ever-increasing black shadow was even better, and so was the replacement of self-despising by self-respect.

19 August

It was truly marvellous to experience energy again, after so many years without it. Having believed that energy was the sole preserve of the young, this was a wonderful benefit that I hadn't expected from quitting smoking. But the greatest benefit of all, which may have been just the accumulation of all the other benefits, was the return of a feeling that I had forgotten ever existed: the sheer joy of living.

20 August

Have you ever written to thank an author after reading a particularly interesting book? I've intended to do so several times, but as with many well-meaning intentions, never actually got round to it. It's a question I often ask new acquaintances, and I have yet to meet a single person who has actually written to thank an author.

21 August

Easyway has received many accolades from the media. But I regard by far the biggest to be the thousands of letters I have received from grateful ex-smokers. The two most common themes of these letters are: 'I can't believe how easy it was!' and, 'Thank you for giving me my life back!'

22 August

What did they mean by, 'Thank you for giving me my life back'? A person who has never smoked would probably interpret it as, 'Thank you for removing the risk of dying from lung cancer.' What they actually mean is, 'Thank you for helping me to escape from domination by this evil weed, from despising myself, and for discovering again the sheer joy of living.'

23 August

Escaping from the nicotine trap is like awakening from a nightmarish, monochrome world of misery and depression, into a sunshine world of health and happiness. It's great to wake up early feeling energetic. It's difficult to describe the joy of waking up, even on a Monday morning, not thinking, 'I wonder what calamities the day will bring?' but rather, 'How marvellous! Another exciting day on this planet'!

24 August

When you feel physically and mentally low, molehills appear to be unscaleable mountains. We all know the truth of the cliché; 'I'd rather be a poor man with good health than a rich man with poor health.' But how often do we find ourselves worrying over something that, even if it materialized, would be no major setback?

25 August

When you feel physically and mentally strong, the reverse happens. Even what would have formerly been major setbacks cease to be problems, and instead become challenges to be met and sur-mounted. They say schooldays are the best days of our lives, although you'll find it hard to convince children.

26 August

I certainly believed it after leaving school. The responsibilities of marriage, setting up home, raising four children, acquiring and holding down a good job, paying the mortgage and keeping a roof over our heads weighed heavily on me. So much so that I look back on those years as the darkest of my life.

27 August

Why should this period have been so depressing? I had a loving, attractive wife, four beautiful and healthy children, a secure, well-paid job and a detached house in a pleasant area. In fact I cannot think of one major problem I had to cope with during a period of nearly 30 years.

28 August

Can it be just coincidence that this was also the period when my life was dominated by nicotine? I extinguished my last cigarette on 15 July 1983. I was 48. I'm now in my seventies. I was also brainwashed to believe that old-age is the most traumatic period of our lives. Can it be coincidence that the last 20+ years have been by far the most enjoyable of my life?

29 August

Has the return of my joy of living been accompanied by the return of my fear of dying? Make no mistake, no way do I want to die, but I don't dwell on the subject as I used to as a child. I'm far too busy enjoying the precious gift of life. I don't know how many more years I'll be blessed with, but what I do know is that I'm going to extract the maximum out of every one of them.

30 August

What a smoker is fighting against when they stop smoking is the feeling of loss. The implication is that smokers are positively doing something they enjoy, so to stop doing it implies deprivation. The reality is quite the opposite. The smoker sacrificed freedom and became a slave when they lit that first cigarette. Losing that slavery is not deprivation, it's liberation.

31 August

Freedom is man's most highly prized goal. For centuries, wars have been fought for the right to be free to worship as you wish. Disabled people fight for the right of access to everyday places so they are free to enjoy their lives to the full. Freedom is precious and worth fighting for. Not one smoker ever dreamt that their freedom would be sacrificed by their addiction. Now it's time to reclaim it.

SEPTEMBER

1 September

Have you ever stopped smoking for a period of time and then started again as a result of a truly stressful event, such as bereavement? If so, you were unlucky. But life is one giant roller coaster and has a knack of throwing up challenges one after another. If, on each occasion, you start smoking again, you will remain a smoker for life.

2 September

Were you ever taught how to live? Did anyone ever tell you how strong our emotions can be? Wouldn't it be nice if we were all taught stress-reducing skills! If we were, perhaps the consumption of cigarettes, alcohol and other addictive drugs would be greatly reduced. Can you remember when, as a child, you decided you wanted to become something special? Your hopes, dreams and desires in a world where anything was possible, the challenge of life itself on both good days and stressful days? These may be distant memories, but you lived life to the full without cigarettes.

3 September

The other problem with starting to smoke again as a result of an upset in life is that when you realize what you've done, you start to feel guilty, thus compounding an already upsetting incident.

4 September

If you want to stop you have to start seeing smoking for what it really is – a trap that is going to do its utmost to prevent you from escaping. It's like an overbearing, devious lover. One who lies and cheats and then begs you not to give them up because, hey, aren't they great and what a great time you have with them. You'd be miserable as hell without them.

5 September

The point is you won't and you've got to start seeing cigarettes in their true light. They aren't your comfort, your helpmate, your true love. They contain a substance to which you are addicted. They are a poisoned chalice. You have to come to terms with this reality if you are to free yourself from their deadly embrace.

6 September

Consider how you would feel if you had just come home from the doctor's and had been told that you have a disease, which is very difficult to cure, and that it could take years and several different treatments before you get rid of it, but that it will always be in you, just dormant?

7 September

How would you feel if you were told that in fact the doctors are wrong? The disease you have is totally curable, and once it's gone it can't come back unless you let it by deliberately infecting yourself again. The cure is immediate. You would be delighted and champing at the bit to get started.

8 September

Nicotine addiction is a disease! I don't just mean it can cause other diseases like cancer, arteriosclerosis, emphysema, asthma, bronchitis or angina. I mean that if you've been fooled into consuming a powerful poison on a regular basis, without receiving any benefits whatsoever, you are suffering from a disease. In fact the disease you are suffering from just happens to be the Number 1 killer disease in western society.

9 September

Perhaps you question this concept. If so, ask yourself whether you regard alcoholism as a pleasure and/or crutch or as a disease. Do you see a heroin addict as someone enjoying and in control of their 'habit', or as someone suffering from a disease? Perhaps it will help to focus your mind if I inform you that fewer than 300 people a year die from heroin addiction in the UK whereas over 2,000 people die every week from nicotine addiction. And that's just in the UK. Worldwide, over 5,000,000 smokers die every year as a direct result of their smoking.

10 September

You have been suffering from the smoking disease. You have had this disease for the number of years you have for a very simple reason: you didn't know how to stop smoking. Now you do.

11 September

The cure for this disease has been around for the last 22 years and yet is taking its time to be recognized by the medical authorities simply because they still think traditionally in terms of curing smokers. We have seen time and time again that their methods don't work. We at Allen Carr have seen time and time again that our method does.

12 September

There is no such thing as a confirmed smoker. Everyone has the ability to change the way they think and behave. The trick is to never take your eye off the ball. Always think consciously about the subject of cigarettes.

13 September

We are aware that we need to perform some functions with our conscious mind and then we carry them out subconsciously. For the smoker smoking is part of this conscious/subconscious pattern of daily living. We know we want a cigarette and respond, but we are never completely conscious of each lungful of smoke we inhale. If we were, we would feel uncomfortable.

14 September

When we become conscious of our smoking we feel awkward, especially if we are in the company of non-smokers. We try to exhale to the side to avoid blowing smoke into their faces. What sort of activity is it that when we are conscious of it, we become embarrassed, and when we can't engage in it we get into a panic?

15 September

The information we carry in our brains is often stored automatically. We don't consciously analyse a lot of what comes in, because at the time it's received it has no bearing on our everyday functioning. A child may learn that mum or dad seem calmer after a cigarette and will refrain from asking for something until their parent is smoking. That child might well conclude that cigarettes make people calm.

16 September

Have you ever been on holiday as a recently stopped smoker? It's hell if you still believe you enjoy cigarettes. Others light up, and you see them happy and smiling, relaxing and enjoying themselves, and you think, 'They're enjoying themselves, but what have I got? Something's wrong here, they're all happy smoking, I don't want to be a smoker but I'm missing out.' But you're wrong. You are responding habitually. Take time to analyse the situation. They're not happy because they smoke, they're happy because they're on holiday. Check with the non-smokers for reassurance.

17 September

Being a smoker is like carrying a ball and chain around
with you. You never escape from its heavy weight. At
times you are convinced it is of great assistance. Only
when you open your eyes and see the true situation
will you appreciate that it is the Number 1 drag in
your life.

18 September

What prevents you from seeing cigarettes as that ball and chain is your false perception, caused by the brainwashing you have undergone from the moment you lit your first cigarette. Once you remove the brainwashing, you will enjoy all aspects of your life more. You will also be better equipped to handle any situation, including stress, without your ball and chain.

19 September

You have nothing to fear from not using nicotine. Not using it makes absolute sense. Far from sinking into oblivion, you will rise to the surface again, out of the trap, and return to the state of equilibrium you once knew. Easyway changes your perspective, because it is based on facts about smoking, not fiction. It's the key that will prise open the door of the prison that is confining you.

20 September

The medical experts tell us that currently every other smoker has their life cut short because they smoke. Let me hasten to say that I don't believe the medical experts. Am I now telling you that smoking doesn't shorten your life? Of course not! What I'm telling you is that it shortens every smoker's life. Use your common sense. If you never changed the oil or the oil filter in your car, are you so stupid that you wouldn't realize the engine's life would be shortened?

21 September

Do we really need medical experts to create tables of the life expectancy based on a 40-year-old smoking a packet a day? Isn't it blatantly obvious from the coughing fit, the feeling of nausea and the foul taste, that whatever intelligence created us, it no more intended us to silt up our bodies with cancerous fumes than a car manufacturer intends us to top up our petrol engine with diesel?

22 September

Perhaps you think I'm sneakily returning to the doctors' theme of, 'Stop smoking because it's killing you.' Not so. This is part of the mind-opening process. We worry dirty oil in our car engine, yet treat the vehicle on which we are totally dependent for the length and quality of our lives with less respect than an old banger.

23 September

The dirty oil can be changed. The human body has the ability to cleanse itself and does so whenever necessary. It's detoxing abilities are 100 times more efficient when it isn't being overloaded with the poison nicotine. How an individual responds to this brief period of recovery is different in each case. Some experience an immediate boost in energy; others feel tired for a short while. Some experience sleep difficulties, which are not insomnia, but an excess of energy. Whatever the symptoms, the body finds its own balance very quickly.

24 September

Now there are certain matters which I must clarify. I promised to explain why some cigarettes appear to taste better than others. Let's use the classic example, the one after a meal, particularly after the evening meal.

25 September

Work for the day is over and you're feeling relaxed. That cigarette will appear to taste even better if you are celebrating with your friends at your favourite restaurant, particularly if they are treating you. On such occasions, non-smokers are on a complete high. But a smoker who isn't able to smoke after a meal isn't on any high at all. So the difference between smoking that cigarette or not isn't just relieving the itch, but the difference between being on a high or being miserable.

26 September

You will find that all the so-called special cigarettes come after a period of abstinence: after exercise, after a break, the first of the day, after sex, and so on. This confirms that the only pleasure any smoker gets from lighting up a cigarette is to end the irritation of craving it. This is because each cigarette creates the irritation, and the one thing that will prolong it throughout your life is more nicotine. The pleasure is an illusion.

27 September

There are many pathetic aspects to nicotine addiction. Having failed so miserably to 'give up' when using 'willpower' methods, I have nothing but admiration for ex-smokers who've managed to do so. But it saddens me when one of them says something like, 'I haven't touched a cigarette for over ten years but I still miss one after a meal.'

28 September

Get it clearly into your mind that no one ever enjoys smoking a cigarette. The only reason we believe we do is because when you are in the nicotine trap, you feel miserable without them. We assume it's the same thing. It isn't.

29 September

There are literally millions of these whingeing ex-smokers who not only perpetuate the belief that they once got great pleasure from smoking, but also perpetuate the illusion for existing smokers. But look back on your life. You've smoked literally thousands of those special ones after a meal. How many of them do you actually remember smoking?

30 September

Open your mind, and look back on your life. You'll find the only things you can remember about smoking are how foul those first, experimental cigarettes tasted, or being miserable because you weren't allowed to smoke, or coughing up your lungs because you were smoking. Those whingeing ex-smokers mope for a situation that never existed.

OCTOBER

1 October

One of our body's survival mechanisms is a built-in device that prevents it from recalling or re-living pain. We know we must have experienced pain, we may even bear the scars, but we are programmed to forget it. If we weren't, the human race would die out. And so it is with misery and despair. We know we had a hard time but we forget the strength of the actual emotions. All smokers live in various stages of despair and misery. Just because we can't recall it accurately after we have given up doesn't mean it didn't exist. It is guaranteed to return if you take up smoking again.

2 October

To help keep your eye on the reality of what it means to be a smoker and why you are so desperate to escape, it helps to write it down. In other words capture your own thoughts and feelings right now, how miserable you feel, how worried you are about being a smoker, and keep it safe in your passport or wallet where you will be able to remind yourself in your own words of what you've escaped from.

3 October

You might wonder how you can immediately stop craving cigarettes when millions of smokers have abstained for years and are still moping. This is the most important message I have for you. I've described the two monsters. The 'little monster' never craves cigarettes. All it does is create an empty, insecure feeling inside your body which you know as: 'I need or want a cigarette.'

4 October

If you don't understand the nicotine trap, you will start to crave a cigarette. The craving is the 'big monster' or the brain-washing. You will then be in a most unenviable situation. Part of your brain will not want to give in, and another part will want to satisfy the craving. With Easyway, because you understand the nature of the trap, the 'big monster' no longer exists, so no way will you start to crave a cigarette.

5 October

Do you remember the tale of Rumpelstiltskin? When the girl didn't know his name she was terrified. Once she did, the situation reversed. He was no longer controlling her, she was now controlling him. For a few days after extinguishing your final cigarette, you might still get the feeling of wanting a cigarette. Instead of pining for one, just stop and think: 'This isn't a pleasant feeling, this is what smokers suffer throughout their smoking lives. Isn't it great? I've no need to feed the 'little monster' ever again.'

6 October

Now you might be wondering how long it takes for the 'little monster' to die. I can't answer that question. But it doesn't matter. The 'little monster' is so slight that we suffer it throughout our smoking lives without even realizing it exists. It gets no worse when we quit. So where's the problem?

7 October

Of course this does create a problem for smokers using a 'willpower' method. Because the 'little monster' is indistinguishable from a hunger for food or normal feelings of stress, whenever they are hungry or under stress, their brains still crave a cigarette.

8 October

With a 'willpower' method the smoker's brain is obsessed with the topic of smoking. Because part of their brain wants to light up, they try to distract their minds from the subject. If ever you've found it difficult to sleep at night, you'll know that the more you worry about it, the more difficult it is to get to sleep.

9 October

The so-called experts claim it's marijuana that gets youngsters into heavier drugs. Nonsense! We are brainwashed from birth to believe that we are weak and that we need some prop or crutch both to enjoy life and to handle stress. We are also brainwashed to believe that nicotine and alcohol will fill the void.

10 October

Be absolutely clear in your mind, neither nicotine nor alcohol fills a void. On the contrary, they create one. Before we fall into either of these traps we can both enjoy life and cope with stress without cigarettes, booze or any other drugs. It is not only imperative to understand that smoking provides no pleasure or crutch whatsoever, but to realize that you don't need to find a substitute for it.

11 October

When we 'give up' smoking, we tend to search for a substitute to take its place. So what we are actually searching for is a magic pill that relieves boredom and stress, aids relaxation and concentration, and doesn't injure our health or cost a fortune. If you ever find such a pill, please let me know! But don't waste your time searching for it. If it existed, we'd all be using it.

12 October

Usually, the nearest we can get to this ideal is to chew gum or suck boiled sweets. If you've ever tried the gum-chewing, you will know that after a few hours, your jaw will be aching and your brain will be saying, 'I'd love a cigarette.' If you've tried sucking boiled sweets, you'll know that after the first three, they'll taste sickly, will coat your teeth and tongue with sugar, ruin your appetite and make you put on weight.

13 October

When you get over a bout of flu, do you search for another disease to take its place? Of course you don't. You are just grateful to be back to normal health. The mere search for a substitute is an admission that you are making a sacrifice. Who wants or needs a substitute for the Number 1 killer disease in western society?

14 October

Can you believe that the medical 'experts' not only recommend a substitute, but actually recommend as a substitute the drug that you are addicted to? It's called Nicotine Replacement Therapy. If the nicotine trap is the biggest confidence trick in the history of the planet, the 'expert' cure, NRT, must come a close second.

15 October

NRT comes in the form of gum, patches, nasal sprays, inhalators, etc. Would you regard it as scientific for a doctor to say, 'Don't smoke heroin, smoking is dangerous. Instead, inject it into a vein'?

16 October

The basis of NRT is that smoking is dangerous, so instead absorb nicotine through your mouth, skin or nose. Even the name is a misnomer. It's the opposite of nicotine replacement, it's nicotine continuation. And it offers no therapy whatsoever.

17 October

Like most things the so-called experts recommend, NRT sounds logical. The theory is that when you try to 'give up' smoking, you have two powerful enemies to defeat: breaking the habit and the terrible physical withdrawal pains. If you were a contender for the world heavyweight boxing championship, your chances of defeating Mike Tyson or Lennox Lewis in their prime would be slim. Your chances of taking them both on at the same time and winning would be non-existent.

18 October

So, it seems not just logical, but plain commonsense, first to extinguish what you hope will be your final cigarette and, while you are breaking the habit, to keep the body supplied with nicotine. Once you've broken the habit, you can then gradually wean yourself off the nicotine.

19 October

But it only sounds logical if you don't understand the nature of the nicotine trap. The theory behind NRT is based on two fallacies that we've already addressed: there are no powerful physical withdrawal pains from nicotine, and smoking isn't a habit. The real truth is that smoking is nothing more nor less than a method of supplying nicotine addicts with their drug.

20 October

In fact there *are* two enemies to defeat. The first is the 'little monster'. Far from being powerful, it is so slight that billions of smokers have lived and died without even being aware it existed. Fortunately it gets no worse when you extinguish your final cigarette. The second I refer to as the 'big monster': the brainwashing – the belief that we get some genuine crutch or pleasure from smoking and that it is difficult to quit.

21 October

It is the 'big monster' that makes it difficult, if not impossible, to quit. By searching for a substitute you are effectively confirming that you are making a sacrifice and so keeping the 'big monster' alive. If you are using NRT, you are actually keeping both monsters alive.

22 October

The nicotine trap is ingenious. Fortunately Easyway is more so. The only problem is to remove the brainwashing and we do that before extinguishing the final cigarette. This is what this diary has been all about. If you have opened your mind and followed all the instructions, you will soon be a happy non-smoker.

23 October

If you still have the feeling that it will be like climbing Everest, in a way you will be absolutely right. The sense of achievement will be very similar. But the marvellous news is that you can enjoy that feeling immediately, right from the moment you quit. Can you imagine how the Count of Monte Cristo felt, believing he would never escape from that dungeon, to find himself suddenly free?

24 October

That's how I felt when I finally escaped from the nicotine trap. Thousands of ex-smokers have written to me describing similar feelings. Fortunately it's a win-win situation. You'll have the euphoria of the achievement without the hassle of climbing Everest. Open your mind and follow the instructions and it will be like a walk through the park on a pleasant summer evening.

25 October

We have reached a critical stage. Perhaps I've yet to convince you that any smoker can find it easy to quit and that you'll enjoy social occasions more and be better able to concentrate or cope with stress as a non-smoker. If so, don't worry. Some people find it difficult to visualize these things. For them the proof of the pudding is in the eating.

26 October

However, if you have opened your mind and followed the instructions, by now you will have realized that smokers get no genuine pleasure or crutch from smoking and that far from relaxing you, relieving boredom and stress or aiding concentration, it does the complete opposite. If you haven't yet reached that realization, my advice is to re-read the whole diary and ask yourself why not!

27 October

If when you've done that, you still don't understand, try to persuade a close friend or relative to explain it to you. If you are still unable to accept it, you need to read my short book *Allen Carr's Easy Way to Stop Smoking* or attend one of my clinics, details of which appear at the end of this diary. If you have understood, you now need to commit yourself to making a genuine and serious attempt to quit when you finish this book.

28 October

You might regard this as a somewhat superfluous piece of advice. After all, why would you be reading this diary unless you intended to quit? The nicotine trap is ingenious. No one ever chooses to become a smoker, yet the trap is designed to imprison you for life. In order to get free, you need to make a conscious decision to escape. I don't mean at this moment, but when you reach the end of this diary.

29 October

If you cannot make that commitment, what you are actually saying is, 'I fully understand that I am suffering from the Number 1 killer disease in western society and that I get no pleasure or crutch whatsoever from smoking, but I have decided to go on suffering from this disease.'

30 October

If that is your position, I regret that I cannot help you. I suggest that you consult a psychiatrist or, better still, an expert in euthanasia. But surely the drug hasn't reduced you so low that you would consider sacrificing the most precious gift anyone could possibly receive?

31 October

If that's how low the drug has dragged you, you've reached the stage that I once did. What have you got to lose?

NOVEMBER

1 November

From this point on, we are going to stop thinking of 'giving up' and the sacrifice and feeling of doom and gloom that goes with it. Instead, we are going to clear the cobwebs from our minds and see nicotine addiction as it really is.

2 November

I promised you there would be no shock treatment and I've explained how we close our minds to the damage smoking does to our health and wealth. However, once you've made the commitment to quit, there's no question of it being a shock treatment. Instead, it becomes a powerful boost to increase the pleasure of being a non-smoker.

3 November

I used to dismiss the risk of lung cancer with the usual spurious arguments that smokers use: 'I could be knocked down by a bus tomorrow!' Or, 'I believe car exhaust fumes cause more damage!' But would you deliberately step under a bus or deliberately put your mouth over a car exhaust and inhale the fumes?

4 November

Rumours about smokers having limbs amputated because of smoking I dismissed as a rather feeble attempt by the medical profession to frighten me into quitting. From the stains on my teeth it was obvious that my lungs were just as stained, but so what, I couldn't see them and neither could anyone else.

5 November

However, if I had realized that the cumulative effect of my smoking was to gradually gunge up every blood-vessel, to starve every muscle and organ of oxygen and nutrients, and replace them with carbon monoxide and other poisons, I'm sure I would have quit earlier. If you wonder why heavy smokers have grey complexions and dried-up skin, it's not due to lack of sunshine but blocked capillaries.

6 November

I had severe varicose veins and liver spots. I would feel dizzy if I stood up too quickly in the bath, and had a weird sensation in my legs. My wife would massage them every evening. I didn't relate any of these symptoms to smoking, but they all disappeared within a few months of quitting.

7 November

Occasionally I had violent pains in my chest and these I did relate to smoking. I hoped indigestion was causing them but suspected it might be lung cancer. I've not had an attack since I quit, and I assume it was angina. Incredibly, my permanent smoker's cough disappeared after just a few days, and I've not had an attack of asthma or bronchitis since I quit.

8 November

Another myth is that smoking helps to reduce weight. This illusion is created because, when using a 'willpower' method, the majority of smokers tend to put on weight. They do so because they substitute food for nicotine. You might argue that proves it's not a myth. But you only have to look around to see that there's no shortage of overweight smokers. I was one of them.

9 November

According to this myth, as a chain-smoker for nearly a third of a century I should have been as thin as a rake. In fact, I was grossly overweight. I lost two stones within six months of quitting. I have no doubt that my obesity contributed to one or more of the symptoms that I described previously. But since the obesity itself was the result of my smoking, it is correct to attribute them to smoking as well.

10 November

How does smoking contribute to obesity? Because
the 'little monster' is indistinguishable from a hunger
for food. As the body builds an immunity to nicotine,
the empty feeling of withdrawal is only partially
relieved by the cigarette and so smokers tend to try
to fill it with food, not just when they try to 'give up'
but throughout their smoking lives.

11 November

Another reason that smoking tends to increase weight is that smokers tend to avoid activities during which they are not able to smoke, particularly exercise. Although I made no conscious decision, I do not believe it was just coincidence that by my mid-twenties, my one and only sport was golf. I could chain-smoke round the golf course without using too much energy. My non-smoking contemporaries were still playing tennis, squash and golf.

12 November

If you have heard rumours that every cigarette you smoke takes five minutes off your life, or that it takes ten years for the gunge to leave your body, ignore them. They are just more vain attempts by the medical profession to frighten you into 'giving up'. They're wasted on the young, because the young don't even realize they're hooked.

13 November

They're not only wasted, but actually back-fire on older, long-term smokers like me. On 100 a day, it meant I'd lost over eight hours of my life every day. In theory, I was not only already dead, but had I quit then, I'd have had to wait another ten years to get rid of the gunge. Not surprisingly, I gave up even trying to 'give up'!

14 November

The five-minute rule is true. But it's only true if you go on to the bitter end and become one of the statistics. Quit now and you can recover 99 per cent of those five minutes. The gunge never leaves your body completely. Even people who have never smoked have some gunge in their lungs from passive smoking.

15 November

Never forget the incredible strength of the human body. If I'd treated my car like my body, it would have been a write-off within six months. The miracle to me is that I permanently breathed this filthy poison into my lungs non-stop for nearly a third of a century and actually survived. What greater testament do you need to the incredible strength of the human body?

16 November

But you don't have to sit around waiting another ten years. You solve your problem the moment you extinguish the final cigarette. I've just described how quickly I recovered from the damaging effects of my smoking. The beautiful truth is that the unhealthy legacy of smoking leaves the body over the first few days and weeks.

17 November

If you took the attitude, 'I could step under a bus tomorrow' when you were regularly poisoning your body with smoking, there is certainly no reason to alter that attitude once you stop. You can make your life more enjoyable and speed up the process with sensible eating and exercise. But don't make a hassle out of it. The primary object of this diary is to help you to enjoy life more.

18 November

Just as we block our minds to the effects of smoking on our health, so we use the tactics of a double-glazing salesman when considering its effects on our wealth. Ask a simple question like: 'How much is this going to cost?' And you'll get an answer like: 'Only £5 a week.' I estimate that, at current values, I spent over £300,000 on nicotine.

19 November

I have a lovely house, but I spent more money paying for the privilege of breathing those filthy fumes, risking those awful diseases, and having my life controlled by that filthy weed than I did on my house. I can be honest and admit this to myself. But I can only do this because my brain is no longer being controlled by the fear of not being able to enjoy life, concentrate or handle stress without a cigarette.

20 November

If you'd asked me, when I was a smoker, how much I was spending, my answer would have been more evasive than that of the double-glazing salesman. It wouldn't have been £175 a week, or even £25 a day. Both answers would merely have confirmed what I already knew, that I was a fool and should 'give up'. No, I'd have said: 'Only £5 a packet and it's worth every penny.' Just how stupid can you get?

21 November

How much did your first cigarette cost you? As with all types of drug addiction, the usual answer is nothing. Isn't it amazing how friends, even strangers, will offer you drugs absolutely free? My first cigarette was also free in a sense. But what did it really cost?

22 November

That first cigarette effectively cost me £300,000. Had I not smoked the first cigarette, I wouldn't have needed the rest. Do I resent the cost? Not one iota. In fact, the £300,000 was the least of the sacrifices I made. If I were to bear resentment, it would be for the lifetime of slavery, despising myself for spending a fortune on a pastime that I loathed, and for not having the willpower to escape.

23 November

I have no resentment now. I realize that, like you, I was just another innocent victim of this ingenious trap. In fact I'm quite proud, because I was the first to understand the true nature of the trap. Once I understood it, escaping from it was enjoyable. I hope you enjoy escaping just as much as I did.

24 November

Have you been calculating how much that first cigarette cost you? What's the point? Better to calculate what the next cigarette will cost you. It's an easy exercise. According to actuarial tables, on average a smoker can expect to live to 60. If you are 40 and smoke a pack a day, it'll cost you about £36,500!

25 November

That's an awful lot of money. Is there anyone on the planet who will pay £36,500 for just one cigarette? Perhaps you'll be lucky and only live to be 50. In which case that next cigarette will only cost you about £18,000. Well, if you're as rich as Bill Gates, you might not worry about paying £18,000 for one cigarette.

26 November

But supposing you are really unlucky and live to be 100. That next cigarette will cost you around £120,000. Perhaps you feel there's a flaw in my calculations. Aren't I assuming that if you smoke the next cigarette, you'll go on smoking for the rest of your life?

27 November

Wise up! We're not talking about having candyfloss once a year. We're talking about the Number 1 addictive drug in western society. How many years have you been smoking? The greatest ingenuity of the trap is that it's designed to keep you in it until you become just another statistic.

28 November

If you don't want to stop today, what makes you think you'll want to stop tomorrow? Perhaps you think the time isn't quite right. Perhaps you are going through a particularly stressful period at the moment, or you have a particularly enjoyable social occasion, like a holiday, or Christmas or a wedding coming up?

29 November

Isn't this just another example of the trap's ingenuity? Isn't there always a special social occasion or stressful situation to enable us to postpone the 'evil' day? Ask yourself this question: if your child or parent were suffering from an increasingly harmful disease, and you knew of an instant, inexpensive and permanent cure, would you really advise them to wait for any event, social or stressful, before receiving the cure?

30 November

The answer to the previous question is obvious, and
if you are still deliberating, it's because of your fear of
being without cigarettes. But you've had the courage
to come this far and no way are you going to miss out
at this stage.

DECEMBER

I December

Initially, I gave you just **three simple instructions. The first was to cast away all feelings of doom and gloom. The second was to open your mind, and the third was to continue smoking until the ritual of the final cigarette and to smoke each cigarette consciously.**

2 December

If you've reached December following those instructions, you will already realize that you are not smoking because you choose to. Isn't it obvious? If any smoker smoked because they chose to, they could just as easily choose not to.

3 December

The first set of instructions was for reading the diary. They were to enable you to realize that not only is there nothing to 'give up', but that it is easy to become a non-smoker immediately, easily and permanently, after extinguishing, not what you *hope* will be your final cigarette, but what you *know* will be your final cigarette.

4 December

Soon I will be issuing **a new set of instructions** which, if you follow them, will enable you to quit easily and permanently.

5 December

We are nearing the ritual of the final cigarette! You are about to achieve something marvellous. Imagine you are just 100ft below the summit of Everest. The weather is good and the adrenalin is flowing. Nothing can prevent you from achieving your goal. I've said that New Year is the very worst day for smokers to quit, but I'm actually going to advise you to perform that ritual after the clock strikes midnight on 31 December.

6 December

Why is New Year the worst time? Because with all the Christmas and New Year celebrations, even casual smokers feel like chain-smokers and are inspired to quit. As you can feel somewhat low after a particularly good holiday, we tend to suffer a low after the celebrations. At the same time, the 'little monster' is now crying out for food. Even if you have the willpower to abstain during the remainder of the holiday, most ex-smokers, no matter how good their intentions, are back on the weed, if not before, then during the first morning back at work.

7 December

With Easyway the day you quit makes no difference. In fact, I often advise smokers to quit on the very day they think they will find it most difficult. If you not only survive but enjoy that day, from then on the going should be plain sailing. Let me emphasize that it is easy to quit smoking. What Easyway does is to remove the obstacles that make it difficult. All you have to do is to follow the instructions.

8 December

The main obstacle is doubt: hoping to become a non-smoker then waiting to see whether you succeed. You didn't need me to tell you that smokers are mugs. That's why you read the diary in the first place. What you need me to tell you is how to make it easy by following my instructions.

9 December

Having made what you know to be the correct decision, **at midnight on 31 December you are going to smoke your final cigarette and make a solemn vow that you will never crave, let alone smoke, another.** It is imperative that this vow is made not with a sense of sacrifice, loss or deprivation – as in, 'I must never smoke again' – but instead with a feeling of elation at having escaped from the sinister trap – 'Isn't it great! I no longer have to choke myself to death on this addictive poison!'

10 December

Accept that in the first few days your mind might be dominated by the subject of smoking. That's only bad if you want to remain a smoker. But you don't! Nor does any other smoker! Realize the true position: nothing bad is happening; on the contrary, something marvellous is happening. You've finally escaped from the smoking trap.

11 December

Do not wait to become a non-smoker. You become a non-smoker the moment you extinguish your final cigarette.

12 December

Having made what you know to be the correct decision, never question or doubt that decision.

13 December

Never forget that from the moment you extinguish that final cigarette, not only will your physical health rapidly improve, but so will your concentration and your confidence.

14 December

Expect to feel a little strange over the next few days. After all, any major change in our lives takes a bit of getting used to, even changes for the better like a bigger house, a new car or a better-paid job. Even if you do find life a bit strange, remember anything you suffer is not because you quit smoking, but because you started.

15 December

Never forget that smoking confers no advantages whatsoever on you or any smoker.

16 December

Never envy other smokers. They will be envying you. Their grass isn't greener but a dirty brown patch.

17 December

Enjoy breaking the associations; by doing it with a conscious mind you will banish them far more quickly. It takes a few weeks for the brain to lose an old pattern of behaviour, or to acquire a new one. For a while after you have stopped smoking, it is perfectly normal for your brain to remember, and associate certain activities, with a cigarette. This is nothing to worry about; it is subconscious programming that will fade away.

18 December

Accept that there will be good days and bad days to come. The good days will be better and the bad days less bad. Remind yourself at the low times that at least you're not a smoker. Just as smokers have good days and bad days, so will you. But your good days will be better than if you were still a smoker and your bad days won't be as bad.

19 December

Re-read your personal statement on why you were so desperate to escape from the smoking trap or take snippets from it to use as a screen saver.

20 December

Do not attempt to achieve a 'happy medium' by attempting to cut down or control your intake.

21 December

Ignore the advice or helpful tips from friends or experts who contradict these instructions, no matter how impressive they sound.

22 December

Don't try not to think about smoking. If I said 'don't think about Mickey Mouse for five seconds and I'll give you £1 million pounds', you would be able to think of nothing else. Just whenever you do think about smoking, think 'Yippee I'm free!'

23 December

Don't use substitutes – you don't need them. And only change your life because you want to anyway, not because you've quit smoking.

24 December

Don't worry if you occasionally forget that you've quit and find yourself reaching for a packet that is no longer there. This can cause a brief pang, but it is a good sign, it means that for a moment, you'd actually forgotten you'd quit. Which means life does go on without being addicted to the weed.

25 December

A few years ago, I had to lean out of my car window, and I found myself reaching to remove the cigarette that 15 years earlier would have been dangling from my lips. You might think this confirms: 'Once a smoker, always a smoker.' On the contrary, it wasn't an unpleasant experience. I thought, 'Fifteen years earlier, not only would I have had a cigarette dangling from my lips, but the ashtray would have been overflowing and my car would have stunk of stale tobacco!'

26 December

If you follow the instructions, after a few days you'll find yourself in a situation – it might be a social occasion or a moment of stress – which you didn't believe you could enjoy or cope with without a cigarette. And you'll suddenly realize that, not only did you enjoy or cope with the situation, but that you never even thought of lighting up.

27 December

This is what I refer to as the Moment of Revelation. It's the moment when you realize that everything I've been saying is true. Not only that it is easy to quit, but that life is so much more enjoyable free from nicotine slavery. But just as you mustn't wait to become a non-smoker, so **you mustn't wait for the Moment of Revelation. You are already a non-smoker. Just get on with your life.**

28 December

Don't avoid smoking situations or social occasions. You've stopped smoking, not stopped living. Remember you haven't even 'given up' smoking. You certainly haven't given up living. It doesn't matter whether two days from now you're sitting in the solitude of your own home, or celebrating at the most important New Year's party of your life.

29 December

You may be among other smokers who have vowed to quit. There may also be cynical smokers present who are convinced, as I once was, that it's impossible to quit. They'll try blowing smoke in your face, or to take you unawares when they think you're off-guard. When they see that not only are you not bothered by the fact that you don't need to smoke but that you are actually enjoying the process, they'll think you are Superman or Superwoman.

30 December

Providing you follow all the instructions, you'll be feeling like Superman or Superwoman!

31 December

Enjoy your escape! If you drink too much and find you're getting somewhat confused, all you need ever remember is that no one wants their children or parents to fall into the nicotine trap. So if you are ever tempted, either tonight or at any time in the future, just remind yourself of what you instinctively know:

YIPPEE ! I'M A NON-SMOKER!

Allen Carr Contact Information

Head Office 1c Amity Grove, London SW20 0LQ
Tel: +44 (0)20 8944 7761
Email: postmaster@allencarr.demon.co.uk
Web: www.allencarrseasyway.com
The following list gives details for **Allen Carr's Easyway to Stop Smoking Clinics** where we guarantee that you will stop smoking – or your money back. **Allen Carr's Easyway to Stop Drinking** and **Easyweigh to Lose Weight Sessions** are available at selected clinics. Please contact your nearest Allen Carr's Easyway to Stop Smoking Clinic for latest details.

UK

London 020 8944 7761 www.allencarrseasyway.com
Birmingham 0121 423 1227 www.allencarrseasyway.com
Bournemouth 01425 272757 www.allencarrseasyway.com
Brighton 0800 028 7257 www.allencarrseasyway.com
Buckinghamshire 0800 0197 017 www.easywaybucks.co.uk
Bristol & Swindon 0117 950 1441 www.easywaybristol.co.uk
Exeter 0117 950 1441 www.easywayexeter.co.uk
Kent 01622 832 554 www.allencarrseasyway.com
Manchester 0800 804 6796 www.easywaymanchester.co.uk
North East 0191 581 0449 www.easywaynortheast.co.uk
Reading 0800 028 7257 www.allencarrseasyway.com
Scotland 0131 449 7858 www.easywayscotland.co.uk
Southampton 0800 028 7257 www.allencarrseasyway.com
South Wales 0117 950 1441 www.easywaycardiff.co.uk
Staines/Heathrow 0800 028 7257 www.allencarrseasyway.com
Yorkshire 0800 804 6796 www.easywaymanchester.co.uk

Worldwide Clinics

Check for your nearest clinic by visiting www.allencarrseasyway.com
and clicking on "Clinic Locations"
or visit the following websites
Republic of Ireland www.easyway.ie
Australia www.allencarr.com.au
Austria www.allen-carr.at
Belgium www.allencarr.be
Belgium (French) www.allencarr.info
Canada www.allencarrseasyway.ca
Colombia www.esfacildejardefumar.com
Denmark www.easyway.dk
France www.allencarr.fr
Germany www.allen-carr.de
Italy www.easywayitalia.com
Mexico www.allencarr-mexico.com
Netherlands www.allencarr.nl
New Zealand www.easywaynz.co.nz or www.allencarr.co.nz
Norway www.easyway-norge.no
Portugal www.comodeixardefumar.com
South Africa www.allencarr.co.za
Spain www.comodejardefumar.com
Switzerland www.allen-carr.ch
UK www.allencarrseasyway.com
USA www.allencarrusa.com